Latitude and longitude

We use latitude and longitude to locate places on the earth's surface. Lines of **latitude** are imaginary lines. They are numbered in degrees North or South of the equator. Lines of **longitude** are imaginary lines which run from the North to the South Poles. They are numbered in degrees East or West of a line through London known as the Prime Meridian.

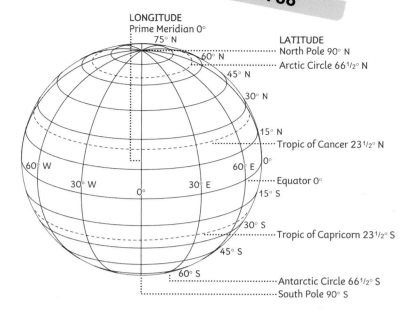

Grid references

Lines of latitude and longitude are used in this atlas to make a grid. The columns are labelled with a letter and the rows with a number. The grid code e.g. B6 can be used to find all places within one grid square.

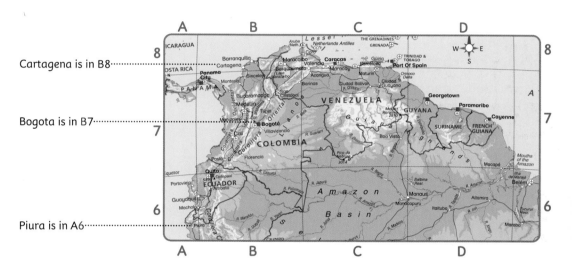

Cartagena is in B8

Bogota is in B7

Piura is in A6

Hemispheres

The equator divides the globe into two halves. All land north of the equator is called the northern hemisphere. Land south of the equator is called the southern hemisphere. 0° and 180° lines of longitude also divide the globes into two imaginary halves, the western and eastern hemispheres.

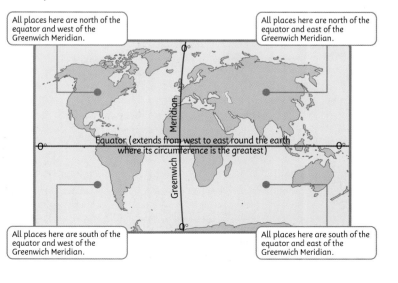

All places here are north of the equator and west of the Greenwich Meridian.

All places here are north of the equator and east of the Greenwich Meridian.

Equator (extends from west to east round the earth where its circumference is the greatest)

Greenwich Meridian

All places here are south of the equator and west of the Greenwich Meridian.

All places here are south of the equator and east of the Greenwich Meridian.

Direction

On most atlas maps you will find a compass. It shows the four compass points North (N), East (E), South (S) and West (W). These help us give more accurate directions.

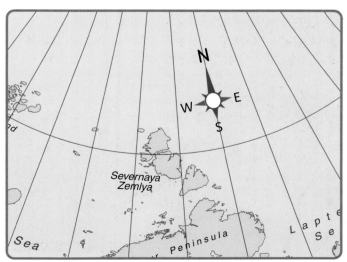

On atlas maps the north point always follows a line of longitude

4 What is an atlas?

Atlas maps

Atlas maps tell us about the various parts of the world. They tell us about different environments in the world.

Some maps show country shapes and where towns are located within the country. These are called political maps.

Some maps show landscapes. They show the physical environment.

Special names and numbers

Special names and numbers are used to label parts of an atlas map.

Title
This names the map area and describes what the map shows.

Page number
This helps you to find out where the map you want is in the atlas.

Locator map
This shows the part of the world covered by the map.

Fact boxes
These contain interesting information about a continent.

Key
This explains what the colours and symbols used on the map represent.

Scale
This explains how large a map is. It helps to work out distances between places. See page 6 to find out more about scale.

Collins Junior
World Atlas

Editorial advisor **Dr. Stephen Scoffham**

Contents

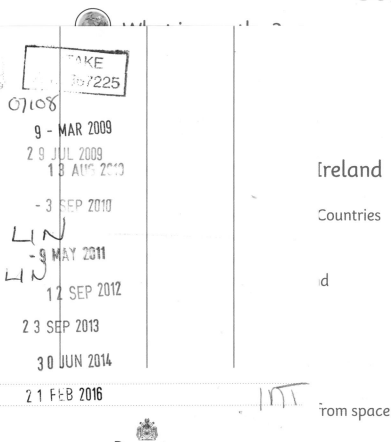

2 What is an atlas?

Globes

Globes are models of the earth. They show the true shape and size of the continents.

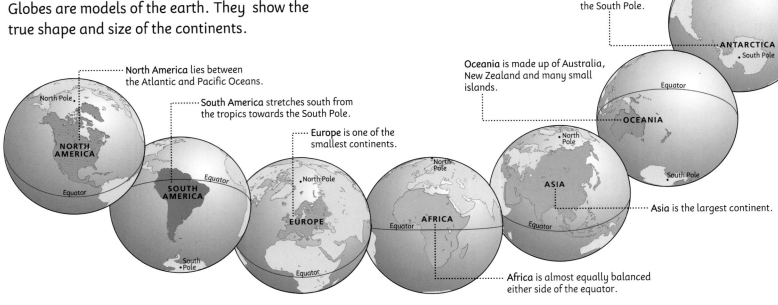

North America lies between the Atlantic and Pacific Oceans.

South America stretches south from the tropics towards the South Pole.

Europe is one of the smallest continents.

Antarctica encircles the South Pole.

Oceania is made up of Australia, New Zealand and many small islands.

Asia is the largest continent.

Africa is almost equally balanced either side of the equator.

Mapping the world

To show the world on a flat map we need to peel the surface of the globe and flatten it out. There are many different methods of drawing atlas maps. These methods are called **projections**.

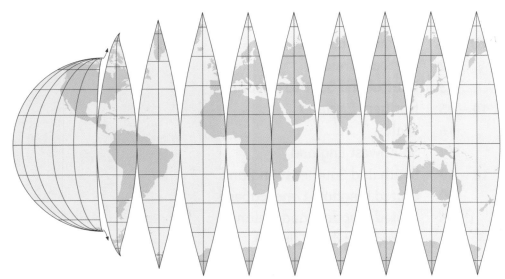

This is how the earth would look if the surface could be peeled and laid flat.

Projections

Map projections change the shape and size of the continents and oceans. The projection used for world maps in this atlas is called Eckert IV.

How the world map looks, depends on which continents are at the centre of the map. Compare the shape of Africa on the maps below to that on the globe.

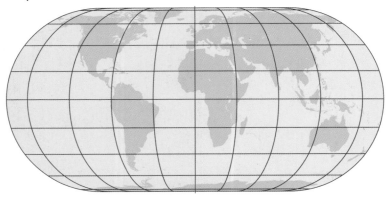

For UK atlases the world would look like this.

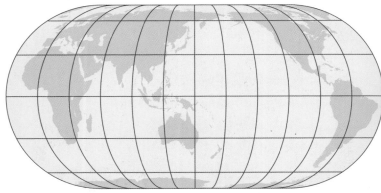

For Australian atlases the world would look like this.

Map symbols

Maps are made up of symbols and names. The symbols can be points, lines or area colours.
A map is complete when the symbols and the names are combined.

Point symbols

- ■ Town stamps
- ▲ Mountain peaks
- ⊕ Airports

Lines

—— Roads	⊣⊢⊣ Railways
▬▬ Country boundaries	
—— Rivers and canals	
—— Coastline	

Area colours

▢ Lake/sea

Land height above sea level in metres

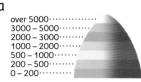

over 5000
3000 – 5000
2000 – 3000
1000 – 2000
500 – 1000
200 – 500
0 – 200

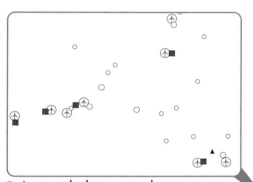

Point symbols are used on a map to show towns, mountain peaks and airports.

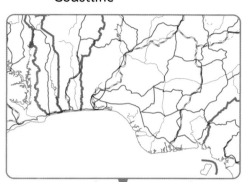

Lines are used an a map to show communications and drainage.

Area colours are used to distinguish the land from the sea and land height above sea level.

Names on atlas maps

The style and size of the type used on maps helps to explain what the name means.

Large bodies of water

PACIFIC OCEAN

Gulf of Guinea

Islands

Cuba

Bioco

Countries

N I G E R I A

BENIN

Large cities

Porto-Novo

Lomé

Small towns

Parakou

Warri

Rivers

Mississippi

Nile

Amazon

Mountain peaks

Mount Cameroon

Everest

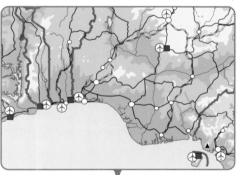

All the symbols are combined to show features and their correct locations.

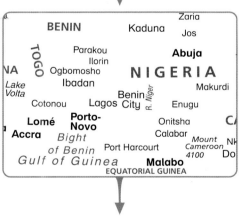

Names are needed to show places and features shown on the map. Only some places and features are named.

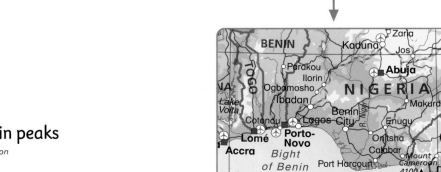

The map is complete when the symbols and the names are combined.

Scale

Maps are much smaller than the regions they show. To
compare the real area with the mapped area you have
to use a scale. Each map in this atlas shows its scale.
This is shown using a scale bar which is explained in words.

E.g.
0   200   400   600   800 km

Scale : One centimetre on this map is the same as 200 kilometres on the ground.

> **Large scale maps
> show smaller areas
> with more detail.** ⟵

LARGE SCALE

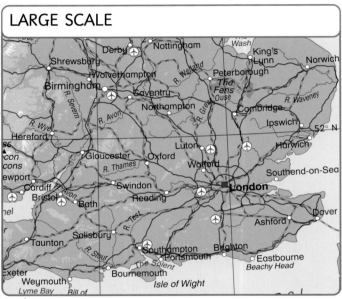

Scale: One centimetre on this map is the same as
40 kilometres on the ground.

0   40   80   120   160   200 km

MEDIUM SCALE

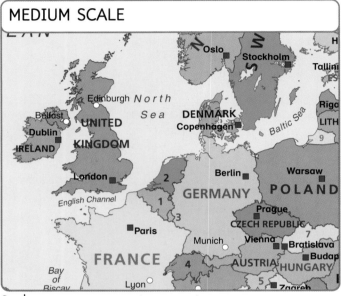

Scale: One centimetre on this map is the same as
250 kilometres on the ground.

0   250   500   750   1000   1250 km

Measuring distance

The scale of a map can be used to measure how far it is
between two places. For example, the straight line distance
between Boa Vista and Cayenne on the map to the right is
5 centimetres.

Look at the ruler.
One centimetre on this map is the same as 200 kilometres on
the ground. The real distance between Boa Vista and Cayenne
is therefore 1000 kilometres (i.e. 5 X 200).

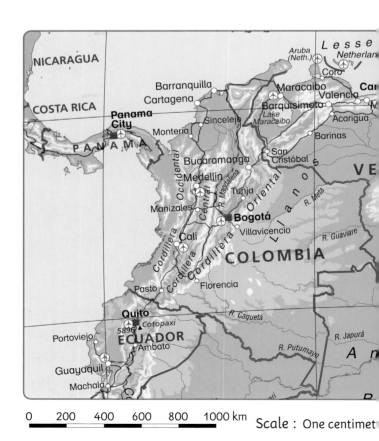

0   200   400   600   800   1000 km   Scale : One centimet

Extend your knowledge and understanding by visiting these websites which provide lots of information and material to help with your homework and projects.

Places
Europe www.eurotales.eril.net
European Union www.europa.eu.int/abc/index_en.htm
CIA Factbook www.cia.gov/cia/publications/factbook
The Thayer Expeditions www.goals.com/thayer/expfrm.htm
Visit Britain www.visitbritain.com
Kids web Japan web-japan.org/kidsweb
Jamaica www.jamaicatravel.com

Climate
World climate statistics www.worldclimate.com

Population
City populations www.citypopulation.de

Geography
Royal Geographical Society www.rgs.org
National Geographic www.nationalgeographic.com

Mountains
Mountains of the world www.peakware.com

Satellite images
Earth Observatory earthobservatory.nasa.gov
Visible Earth visibleearth.nasa.gov
MODIS satellite images modis.gsfc.nasa.gov

Development issues
Global Eye www.globaleye.org.uk

Flags
Flags of the world www.theodora.com/flags

International organisations
ActionAid International www.actionaid.org
The Commonwealth www.youngcommonwealth.org
Christian Aid www.globalgang.org.uk
United Nations www.cyberschoolbus.un.org
UNICEF www.unicef.org
Save the Children www.savethechildren.org
Greenpeace www.greenpeace.org/international

Small scale maps show larger areas with less detail.

SMALL SCALE

Scale: One centimetre on this map is the same as 800 kilometres on the ground.

0   800   1600   2400   3200 km

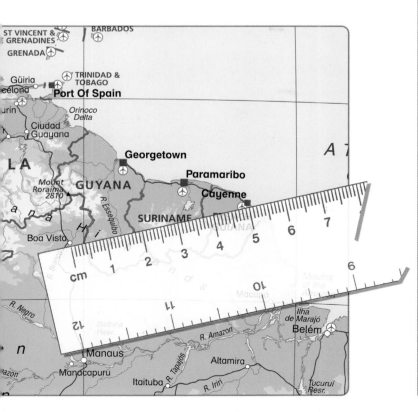

map is the same as 200 kilometres on the ground.

The islands to the northwest of mainland Europe are divided between two countries – the United Kingdom and Ireland. The largest island, called Great Britain, is the eighth largest in the world.

Key to symbols

- ■ Capital city
- ○ Main city/town
- ○ Other city/town
- ── Country boundary
- ── Road
- ── Railway
- ✈ Airport
- Lake
- ～ River
- ▲ *Ben Nevis* 1344 Mountain and height in metres

Land height above sea level in metres

over 5000
3000 – 5000
2000 – 3000
1000 – 2000
500 – 1000
200 – 500
0 – 200

Land below sea level

Shetland Islands — Mainland, Lerwick, Sumburgh Head, Fair Isle

ATLANTIC OCEAN

Orkney Islands — Mainland, Hoy, Kirkwall, Pentland Firth, Duncansby Head

Cape Wrath, Butt of Lewis, Thurso, Wick, Duncansby Head

Outer Hebrides, Isle of Lewis, Stornoway, Tarbert, Harris, North Uist, South Uist, St Kilda, The Minch

Loch Shin, Ullapool, North West Highlands, Loch Ness, Inverness, Moray Firth, R. Spey, R. Don, R. Dee, Aberdeen, Rattray Head

Skye, Uig, Rum, Cairngorm Mts, Ben Macdui 1309, Grampian Mountains

Inner Hebrides, Coll, Tiree, Mull, Oban, Fort William, Ben Nevis 1344, Loch Tay, Ben More 1174, Loch Lomond, R. Tay, Perth, Dundee, Firth of Tay

Firth of Lorn, Jura, Islay, Stirling, R. Forth, Firth of Forth

Glasgow, Edinburgh, Ayr, Arran, Mull of Kintyre, Berwick-upon-Tweed, R. Tweed, Cheviot Hills

North Sea

UNITED KINGDOM

Malin Head, Errigal 752, Londonderry, Coleraine, Antrim Hills, R. Bann, Larne, North Channel, Merrick 843, Southern Uplands, R. Nith, Dumfries, Newcastle upon Tyne, Sunderland, Stranraer, Solway Firth, Carlisle, Workington, R. Tyne, R. Tees, Darlington, Middlesbrough

Donegal, Donegal Bay, Lough Neagh, Lower Lough Erne, Enniskillen, Upper Lough Erne, Belfast, Newry, Mourne Mts, Slieve Donard 852, Dundalk, Scafell Pike 977, Lake District, Isle of Man, Douglas, North York Moors, R. Derwent, Scarborough, Flamborough Head

Ballina, Sligo, Lough Conn, Lough Mask, Achill Island, Westport, Lough Corrib, Galway, Galway Bay, R. Shannon, R. Moy, R. Suck, Lough Ree, R. Boyne, Drogheda, Dundalk Bay, Irish Sea, Morecambe Bay, Blackpool, Preston, R. Ribble, Bradford, Leeds, Huddersfield, York, Kingston upon Hull, Grimsby, Spurn Head

IRELAND, Lough Derg, R. Barrow, R. Nore, R. Suir, R. Liffey, Dublin, Anglesey, Holyhead, Caernarfon, Snowdon 1085, Liverpool, R. Mersey, Manchester, Sheffield, Doncaster, Lincoln, Chester, Crewe, Stoke-on-Trent, R. Trent, R. Dee

Wicklow Mts, Wicklow, Wicklow Head, Derby, Nottingham, The Wash

Limerick, R. Shannon, Cardigan Bay, Aberystwyth, Cambrian Mountains, Shrewsbury, Wolverhampton, R. Welland, King's Lynn, Norwich, Peterborough, The Fens, Ouse, R. Waveney

Tralee, Carrantuohill 1041, R. Suir, Wexford, Rosslare, St George's Channel, St David's Head, Fishguard, Pembroke, Brecon Beacons 886, Hereford, R. Wye, Birmingham, Coventry, Northampton, R. Avon, R. Great Ouse, Cambridge, Ipswich

Cork, Cape Clear, R. Lee, R. Blackwater, Waterford, Celtic Sea, Swansea, Newport, Cardiff, Bristol, Gloucester, R. Thames, Oxford, Luton, Watford, Harwich, Southend-on-Sea

Exmoor, Bristol Channel, Taunton, R. Exe, Salisbury, R. Test, Reading, London, Ashford, Dover

Bodmin Moor, Dartmoor 619, R. Tamar, Exeter, Weymouth, Lyme Bay, Bill of Portland, Bournemouth, Southampton, Portsmouth, The Solent, Isle of Wight, Brighton, Eastbourne, Beachy Head

Penzance, Land's End, Isles of Scilly, Lizard Point, Plymouth, English Channel, Dieppe, FRANCE

Pennines, R. Darwent

Four countries make up the United Kingdom or UK. They are England, Scotland, Wales and Northern Ireland. The Isle of Man and Channel Islands are also part of the UK but have their own laws.

Key to symbols

- Countries
- ■ Capital city
- ● National capital
- ○ Important city/town

United Kingdom

Scotland

Northern Ireland

Wales

England

Ireland

ATLANTIC OCEAN

North Sea

Shetland Islands

Orkney Islands

Outer Hebrides

Inverness
Aberdeen
Fort William
SCOTLAND
Dundee
Glasgow
Edinburgh

Londonderry
NORTHERN IRELAND
Belfast

IRELAND
Dublin ■

Irish Sea

Isle of Man

Newcastle upon Tyne
Middlesbrough

UNITED

Blackpool
Preston
Bradford Leeds
York
Liverpool Manchester Sheffield

KINGDOM

Stoke-on-Trent Derby Nottingham
ENGLAND Norwich
Wolverhampton Leicester
Birmingham Cambridge
Coventry Ipswich
WALES
Oxford
Swansea London ■ Southend-on-Sea
Cardiff Bristol Reading
BELGIUM
Southampton Brighton
Portsmouth
Bournemouth
Plymouth Torquay
English Channel
Channel Islands FRANCE

The U.K. government makes laws in the Houses of Parliament in London.

50   100   150   200   250   300 km

Scale : One centimetre on this map is the same as 50 kilometres on the ground.

The Scottish highlands are the emptiest part of the UK. There are many small islands around the coast. They are linked to the mainland by ferry.

Scotland has many mountains. Those which are over 3000 feet (914 m) high are called Munros. This one is in Glen Coe near Ben Nevis.

Key to symbols

- ○ Main city/town
- ◦ Other city/town
- — Road
- ┼ Railway
- ⊕ Airport
- ⬭ Lake
- ⌇ River
- ▲ Ben Nevis 1344 Mountain and height in metres

Land height above sea level in metres

- over 1500
- 1000 – 1500
- 900 – 1000
- 500 – 900
- 200 – 500
- 100 – 200
- 0 – 100

ATLANTIC OCEAN

58° N

57° N

9° W

8° W

7° W

6° W

5° W

Outer Hebrides

Flannan Isles

St Kilda

Scarp

Great Bernera

Loch Langavat

Lewis

Stornoway

Butt of Lewis

Port of Ness

Tolsta Head

Port Nan Giùran

Eye Peninsula

Kebock Head

Clishham 799

Tarbert

Scalpay

Harris

Pabbay
Berneray

Sound of Harris

Rodel

North Uist

Lochmaddy

Monach Islands

Benbecula

South Uist

Beinn Mhor 620

Lochboisdale

Sound of Barra

Eriskay

Barra

Sheabhal 383

Vatersay

Castlebay

Sandray

Mingulay

Little Minch

Rubha Hunish

Loch Snizort

Dunvegan

Uig

The Storr 719

Portree

Raasay

Skye

Rona

Cuillin Hills 993

Sgurr Alasdair

Blaven 928

Soay

Scalpay

Canna

Cuillin Sound

Ardvasar

Rum

Askival 812

Eigg

Muck

Inner Hebrides

Coll

Ben Hogh 104

Arinagour

Tiree

Scarinish

Point of Ardnamurchan

Tobermory

Loch Frisa

Morvern

Sound of Mull

Lochaline

Loch Sunart

Cape Wrath

Durness

Kinlochbervie

Handa Island

Scourie

Foinaven 915

Point of Stoer

Lochinver

Loch Assynt

Ben More Assynt 998

Summer Isles

The Minch

Ullapool

Loch Broom

An Teallach 1062

Fionn Loch

Rubha Reidh

Gairloch

Loch Ewe

Loch Maree

Sgurr Mor 1110

WESTER ROSS

L. Torridon

Inner Sound

Sound of Sleat

Kyle of Lochalsh

Kyleakin

Carn Eighe 1183

Glen Affric

R. Orrin

Sgurr a'Choire 1083

Loch Monar

North West

Glen Shiel

Loch Cluanie

R. Garry

R. Moriston

Ladhar Bheinn 1020

Loch Hourn

Loch Quoich

Loch Arkaig

Mallaig

Loch Morar

Sound of Arisaig

Sgurr Dhomhnuill 888

Gulvain 983

Loch Shiel

Fort William

Ben Nevis 1344

Loch Leven

Glen Coe

Bidean nam Bian 1150

Loch Linnhe

Loch Etive

Glen Garry

Augu

S

Kinloc

Scale bar: 0 — 25 — 50 — 75 km

Northern Scotland map

Orkney Islands

Fair Isle
Papa Westray
Westray
North Ronaldsay
N. Ronaldsay Firth
Eday
Sanday
Rousay
Westray Firth
Stronsay
Brough Head
Stronsay Firth
Shapinsay
Stromness
Loch of Harray
Kirkwall
Mainland
Skaill
Ward Hill
479
Scapa Flow
Burray
Hoy
Flotta
South Ronaldsay
Burwick
Pentland Firth
59° N
Dunnet Head
John o'Groats
Duncansby Head
Thurso B.
Dounreay
Thurso
Loch Watten
Sinclair's Bay
Tongue
Bettyhill
R. Wick
CAITHNESS
Loch Loyal
Wick
ERLAND
961
Ben breck
Loch Rimsdale
R. Thurso
R. Helmsdale
Lybster
DS
Helmsdale
NORTH
Lairg
R. Brora
SEA
Brora
58° N
Golspie
Dornoch Firth
Tarbat Ness
Tain
Moray Firth
Invergordon
Cromarty Firth
Lossiemouth
Cullen
Macduff
Fraserburgh
Black Isle
Kinloss
Buckie
Banff
Rattray Head
Dingwall
Elgin
Fochabers
Crimond
Conon Bridge
Fortrose
Forres
Knock Hill
R. Deveron
Moray Firth
Nairn
Rothes
R. Isla 430
Turriff
Mintlaw
Inverness
Keith
Peterhead
R. Findhorn
Dufftown
R. Ness
Huntly
Cruden Bay
R. Nairn
Grantown-on-Spey
STRATHBOGIE
Oldmeldrum
R. Ythan
Ellon
TLAND
Strathspey
R. Bogie
Inverurie
R. Don
Aviemore
Kintore
Dyce
dhlaith Mountains
Cairn Gorm 1245
R. Avon
Aberdeen
Kingussie
Cairngorm Mts
Newtonmore
Ben Macdui 1309
Aboyne
R. Dee
ggan
R. Spey
Braemar
Ballater
Banchory
Dalwhinnie
1155
Stonehaven
L. Ericht
Carn nan Gabhar 1121
Lochnagar
North R. Esk
Inverbervie
r
Glenshee
Grampian Mountains
Laurencekirk
Blair Atholl
Backwater Reservoir
South R. Esk
L. Rannoch
1083
Schiehallion
R. Isla
Brechin
Montrose
Loch Tummel
R. Tummel
Pitlochry
Kirriemuir
och
R. Lyon
R. Tay
Blairgowrie
Forfar
Ben Lawers 1214
Aberfeldy
Coupar Angus
Strathmore
Sidlaw Hills
Arbroath
Carnoustie

Shetland Islands (inset)

Herma Ness
Unst
Point of Fethaland
Yell Sound
Fetlar
Ronas Hill 450
Yell
St. Magnus Bay
Sullom Voe
Toft
Out Skerries
Muckle Roe
Whalsay
Papa Stour
Mainland
Lerwick
Foula
Shetland Islands
Bressay
60° N
Sumburgh
Sumburgh Head
Fair Isle

Platforms in the North Sea are used to bring oil ashore from rocks under the ocean.

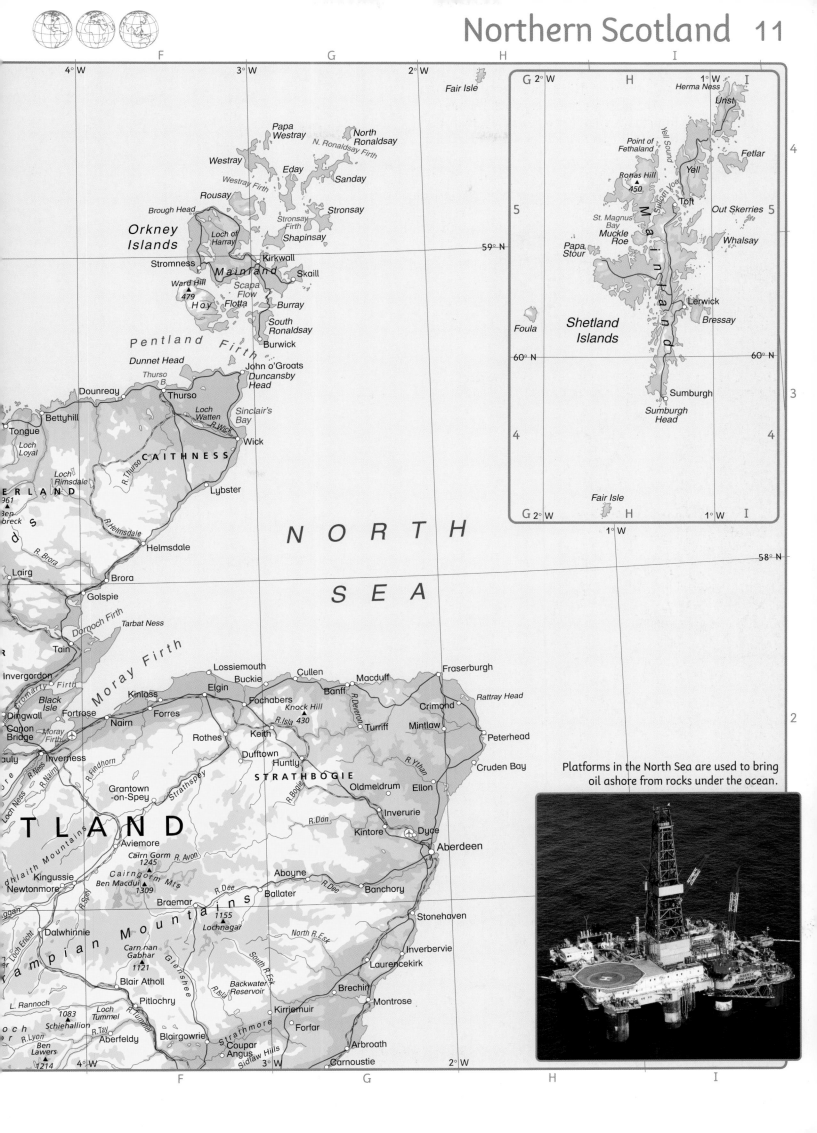

Northern Ireland is the smallest country in the UK. Most places are less than 100 km from the capital, Belfast. Lough Neagh is a large lake in the middle of Northern Ireland.

After many years of fighting, Catholics and Protestants now work together to govern Northern Ireland from Stormont.

N W E S

6° W
5° W

Eigg
Loch Morar
Gulvain 983
Creag Meagaidh 1130
Muck
Loch Shiel
Sgurr Dhomhnuill 888
Fort William 1344
Ben Nevis
Ben Alder 1148
Point of Ardnamurchan
Ben Hogh 104
Arinagour
Tobermory
Loch Sunart
Morvern
Loch Linnhe
Lochaline
Kinlochleven
Loch Leven
Glen Coe
Grampi
1150
Bidean nam Bian
Coll
Treshnish Isles
Loch Frisa
Sound of Mull
Lismore
SCO
Scarinish
Ulva
Craignure
Loch Etive
Ben Cruachan 1126
Rannoc Moor
Tiree
Staffa
Ben More 966
Mull
Oban
R. Orchy
1130 Crianlarich R.I
The Trossa
Iona
Fionnphort
Firth of Lorn
1174 Ben More
Ben Lui
56° N
Luing
Loch Awe
974 Loch Katrine
Colonsay
Scarba
Argyll
Ben Lomond
Loch Long
Loch Lom
Oronsay
Jura
Lochgilphead
Garelochhead
Loch Fyne
Helensburgh
Beinn an Oir 785
Dunoon
Greenock
Dum
Port Askaig
Sound of Jura
Tarbert
Port Glasgow
Islay
Rothesay
Wemyss Bay
Renfre
Bowmore
Beinn Bheigeir 491
Gigha
Kennacraig
Bute
Largs
Millport
Great Cumbrae
Paisley
Barrhea
Loch Indaal
Port Ellen
Kilbrannan Sound
Firth
New Mec
Dalry
Ste
Goat Fell 874
Ardrossan
Mull Of Oa
Kintyre
Arran
Brodick
Lamlash
of Clyde
Irvine
Troon
Prestwick
Kil

Malin Head
Inishtrahull
Machrihanish
Campbeltown
Ayr
Cu
Rathlin Island
Mull of Kintyre
Fair Head
Culzean Bay
R.
Inishowen
Giant's Causeway
Magilligan Point
Portrush
Bushmills
Ballycastle
Ailsa Craig
Girvan
Slieve Snaght 675
Moville
Portstewart
Coleraine
R. Bush
Ballantrae
Merric 843
Lough Swilly
Buncrana
Lough Foyle
Ballymoney
Trostan 554
Garron Point
Milleur Point
Errigal 752
Derryveagh Mts
Letterkenny
Limavady
Londonderry
Dungiven
R. Bann
Antrim Hills
Carntough
North Channel
Cairnryan
Newton Stewart
Stranraer
Wigtown
R. Foyle
R. Deele
Lifford
R. Finn
Strabane
Sawel Mt 683
Sperrin Mts
Maghera
R. Main
Ballymena
Larne
The Rinns of Galloway
Blue Stack Mts
Blue Stack 676
Newtownstewart
Magherafelt
Ballyclare
Island Magee
Luce Bay
Lough Eske
R. Derg
Castlederg
R. Strule
R. Mourne
Antrim
Newtownabbey
Carrickfergus
Drummore
Donegal
NORTHERN
Cookstown
Lough
Crumlin
Belfast Lough
Bangor
Burrow He
Lough Derg
Omagh
IRELAND
Neagh
Belfast
Newtownards
Ballyshannon
Dungannon
Lisburn
Comber
Strangford Lough
Ards Peninsula
IRISH
Bundoran
R. Erne
Lower Lough Erne
Lurgan
Saintfield
Portaferry
Lough Melvin
R. Blackwater
Portadown
Craigavon
R. Lagan
Tullybrack 376
Enniskillen
Armagh
Ballynahinch
Banbridge
R. Bann
Point of A
Manorhamilton
Lisnaskea
Ulster Canal
Monaghan
Newry
Downpatrick
Ardglass
ISLE OF MAN
Lough Gill
R. Shannon
Upper Lough Erne
Clones
Newcastle
Slieve Donard 852
Dundrum Bay
Ramsey Snaefe 625
Cuncagh 667
Lough Oughter
Mourne Mts
Lough Allen
Slieve Anierin 586
Castleblayney
R. Annalee
Warrenpoint
Kilkeel
Peel
Lough Arrow
Lough Key
Cavan
R. Fane
Kilkeel
Port Erin
Do
54° N
Carrick-on-Shannon
Carrickmacross
Dundalk
Calf of Man
Castletown
Boyle
IRELAND
Moyer 341
Kingscourt
Dundalk Bay
Port Erin
Lough Boderg
Lough Gowna
Baillieborough
8° W
7° W
6° W
5° W

Scale : One centimetre on this map is the same as 12.5 kilometres on the ground.

Most people in Scotland live in the central lowlands. The biggest cities, Edinburgh and Glasgow, are less than 70 km apart.

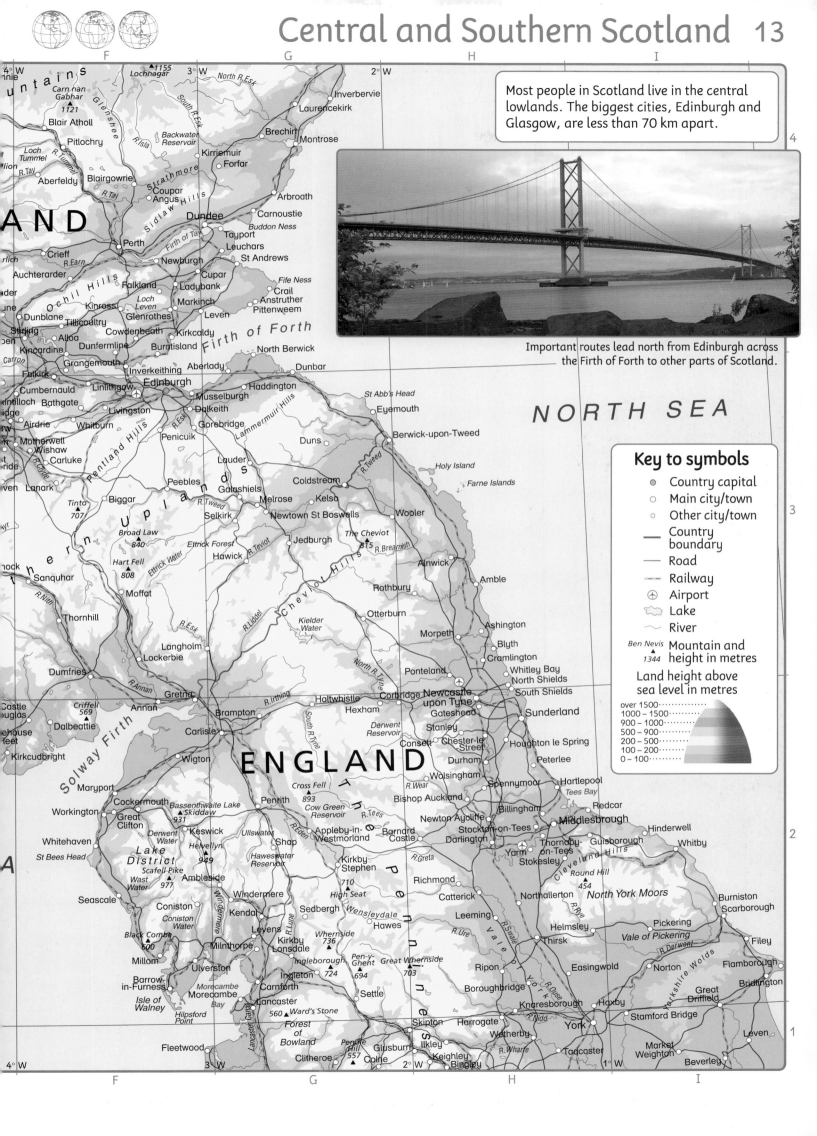

Important routes lead north from Edinburgh across the Firth of Forth to other parts of Scotland.

NORTH SEA

ENGLAND

Key to symbols

- ● Country capital
- ○ Main city/town
- ○ Other city/town
- ── Country boundary
- ── Road
- ── Railway
- ✈ Airport
- Lake
- River

Ben Nevis
▲ Mountain and height in metres
1344

Land height above sea level in metres

over 1500
1000 – 1500
900 – 1000
500 – 900
200 – 500
100 – 200
0 – 100

Place names (as labelled on the map)

Carn nan Gabhar ▲1121, Lochnagar ▲1155, North R. Esk, Inverbervie, Laurencekirk, Blair Atholl, Glenshee, Pitlochry, Backwater Reservoir, R. Isla, Brechin, Montrose, Loch Tummel, R. Tummel, Kirriemuir, Forfar, Aberfeldy, Blairgowrie, R. Tay, Coupar Angus, Sidlaw Hills, Strathmore, Arbroath, Carnoustie, Dundee, Buddon Ness, Crieff, R. Earn, Perth, Tayport, Leuchars, Auchterarder, Newburgh, St Andrews, Cupar, Leven, Ochil Hills, Falkland, Ladybank, Fife Ness, Dunblane, Kinross, Loch Leven, Markinch, Crail, Anstruther, Pittenweem, Stirling, Tillicoultry, Glenrothes, Leven, Alloa, Cowdenbeath, Kirkcaldy, Kincardine, Dunfermline, Burntisland, Grangemouth, Firth of Forth, North Berwick, Falkirk, Inverkeithing, Aberlady, Dunbar, Cumbernauld, Linlithgow, Edinburgh, Haddington, St Abb's Head, Kintilloch, Bathgate, Livingston, Musselburgh, Eyemouth, Airdrie, Whitburn, Dalkeith, Gorebridge, Berwick-upon-Tweed, Motherwell, Penicuik, Lammermuir Hills, Duns, R. Tweed, Holy Island, Wishaw, Carluke, Lauder, Farne Islands, Lanark, Peebles, Galashiels, Coldstream, Kelso, Tinto ▲707, Biggar, R. Tweed, Melrose, Wooler, Southern Uplands, Broad Law ▲840, Selkirk, Newtown St Boswells, The Cheviot ▲815, R. Breamish, Hart Fell ▲808, Ettrick Forest, Ettrick Water, Jedburgh, Hawick, R. Teviot, Alnwick, Sanquhar, Moffat, R. Esk, Cheviot Hills, R. Liddel, Kielder Water, Otterburn, Amble, R. Nith, Thornhill, Rothbury, Morpeth, Ashington, Langholm, Lockerbie, North R. Tyne, Blyth, Cramlington, Dumfries, Ponteland, Whitley Bay, North Shields, R. Annan, Gretna, R. Irthing, Haltwhistle, Corbridge, Newcastle upon Tyne, South Shields, Criffel ▲569, Annan, Brampton, Hexham, Gateshead, Sunderland, Castle Douglas, Carlisle, Derwent Reservoir, Stanley, Dalbeattie, Consett, Chester-le-Street, Houghton le Spring, Kirkcudbright, Wigton, Durham, Peterlee, Maryport, Solway Firth, Wolsingham, Spennymoor, Hartlepool, Cockermouth, Bassenthwaite Lake, Cross Fell ▲893, R. Wear, Tees Bay, Workington, Great Clifton, Skiddaw ▲931, Keswick, Penrith, Cow Green Reservoir, Bishop Auckland, Billingham, Redcar, Whitehaven, Derwent Water, Ullswater, Shap, R. Eden, Appleby-in-Westmorland, Barnard Castle, Newton Aycliffe, Stockton-on-Tees, Middlesbrough, Hinderwell, St Bees Head, Lake District, Helvellyn ▲949, Hawesworth Reservoir, R. Greta, Darlington, Thornaby-on-Tees, Guisborough, Whitby, Scafell Pike ▲977, Ambleside, Kirkby Stephen, Richmond, Yarm, Stokesley, Cleveland Hills, Round Hill ▲454, Seascale, Windermere, High Seat ▲710, Catterick, Northallerton, North York Moors, Burniston, Coniston, Wast Water, Kendal, Sedbergh, Wensleydale, Leeming, R. Rye, Scarborough, Coniston Water, Hawes, R. Ure, Helmsley, Pickering, Black Combe ▲600, Milnthorpe, Whernside ▲736, Vale of Pickering, Filey, Millom, Kirkby Lonsdale, Pen-y-Ghent ▲694, Great Whernside ▲703, Ripon, Easingwold, Norton, Yorkshire Wolds, Flamborough, Ulverston, Ingleborough ▲724, Settle, Boroughbridge, R. Swale, R. Derwent, Bridlington, Barrow-in-Furness, Morecambe, Carnforth, Knaresborough, Haxby, Great Driffield, Isle of Walney, Morecambe Bay, Ward's Stone ▲560, Vale of York, R. Nidd, Stamford Bridge, Hilpsford Point, Lancaster, Ripon, R. Ouse, Leven, Forest of Bowland, Pendle Hill ▲557, Skipton, Harrogate, Wetherby, York, Tadcaster, Market Weighton, Fleetwood, Clitheroe, Glusburn, Colne, Ilkley, Keighley, Bingley, R. Wharfe, Beverley

The Pennine hills run southwards from Scotland through northern England. Old industrial cities such as Manchester, Bradford and Sheffield are found on the edge of the Pennines.

Tourists come to Derwent Water and other parts of the Lake District to enjoy the beautiful scenery.

Scale : One centimetre on this map is the same as 12.5 kilometres on the ground.

0   25   50   75 km

F   G   H   I

2° W   1° W   0°   1° E

NORTH SEA

St Abb's Head
Eyemouth
Berwick-upon-Tweed
R.Tweed
Holy Island
Farne Islands
Wooler
The Cheviot
815
R.Breamish
Alnwick
Rothbury
Amble
Otterburn
Ashington
Morpeth
Blyth
Cramlington
Whitley Bay
Ponteland
North Shields
North R.Tyne
Corbridge
Newcastle upon Tyne
South Shields
whistle
Hexham
Gateshead
Tyne
Sunderland
Derwent Reservoir
Stanley
Chester-le-Street
Consett
Houghton le Spring
Durham
Peterlee
Wolsingham
Spennymoor
R.Wear
Hartlepool
Tees Bay
Cow Green Reservoir
Bishop Auckland
Billingham
Redcar
Newton Aycliffe
Stockton-on-Tees
R.Tees
Middlesbrough
Guisborough Hinderwell
Barnard Castle
Darlington
Thornaby-on-Tees
by-in-morland
Yarm
Whitby
Kirkby Stephen
R.Greta
Stokesley
Cleveland Hills
High Seat 710
Richmond
Round Hill 454
North York Moors
Catterick
Northallerton
R.Rye
Wensleydale
Leeming
Burniston
Hawes
R.Ure
Pickering
Scarborough
R.Swale
Vale of Pickering
Helmsley
Filey
694 Pen-y-Ghent
Great Whernside 703
Thirsk
R.Derwent
Flamborough
Flamborough Head
Settle
Ripon
Boroughbridge
Easingwold
Norton
Bridlington
ENGLAND
Yorkshire Wolds
Bridlington Bay
Skipton
Knaresborough
Haxby
Stamford Bridge
Great Driffield
Harrogate
York
Wetherby
R.Nidd
Glusburn
Ilkley
R.Wharfe
Leven
Pendle Hill 557
Keighley
Bingley
Tadcaster
Market Weighton
Beverley
Aldbrough
Nelson
Shipley
Pudsey
Garforth Selby
South Cave
Bilton
Burnley
Bradford
Leeds
R.Ouse
Brough
Kingston upon Hull
Withernsea
Accrington
Halifax
Batley
Castleford
Howden
Barton-upon-Humber
Patrington
Rawtenstall
Dewsbury
Pontefract
Goole
Immingham
Mouth of The R.Humber
Spurn Head
Littleborough
Wakefield
Thorne
Holderness
Rochdale
South Kirkby
Hatfield
Scunthorpe
Grimsby
Bury
Oldham
Huddersfield
Barnsley
Doncaster
Bottesford
Caistor
Lacebu
Cleethorpes
Manchester
Black Hill 582
Rossington
R.Trent
Sale
Glossop
Rotherham
Maltby
Gainsborough
Louth
Mablethorpe
Stockport
Kinder Scout
High Peak 636
Sheffield
Blyth
Market Rasen
Wilmslow
Chapel-en-le-Frith
Worksop
Wragby
Dronfield
Shining Tor 599
Buxton
Staveley
Bolsover
Lincoln
Heighington
Horncastle
Chesterfield
R.Meden
Tuxford
Sherwood
Spilsby
Skegness
R.Dove
Matlock
Mansfield
Sutton in Ashfield
Sherwood Forest
Newark-on-Trent
R.Bain
West Fen
East Fen
Wainfleet All Saints
Biddulph
Alfreton
Belper
Ripley
Eastwood
Southwell
Sleaford
Holland Fen
Wrangle
Kidsgrove
Leek
Stoke-on-Trent
Ashbourne
Ilkeston
Long Bennington
R.Witham
Boston
Hunstanton
Wells-next-the-Sea
Cromer
Cheadle
Derby
Nottingham
West Bridgford
Bingham
Grantham
Sutterton
R.Welland
The Wash
Fakenham
North Walsham
Long Eaton
Uttoxeter

Key to symbols

- ⬤ Country capital
- ◯ Main city/town
- ◦ Other city/town
- Country boundary
- Road
- Railway
- ✈ Airport
- Lake
- River
- ▲ Scafell Pike 977   Mountain and height in metres

Land height above sea level in metres

over 1500
1000 – 1500
900 – 1000
500 – 900
200 – 500
100 – 200
0 – 100

53° N
55° N

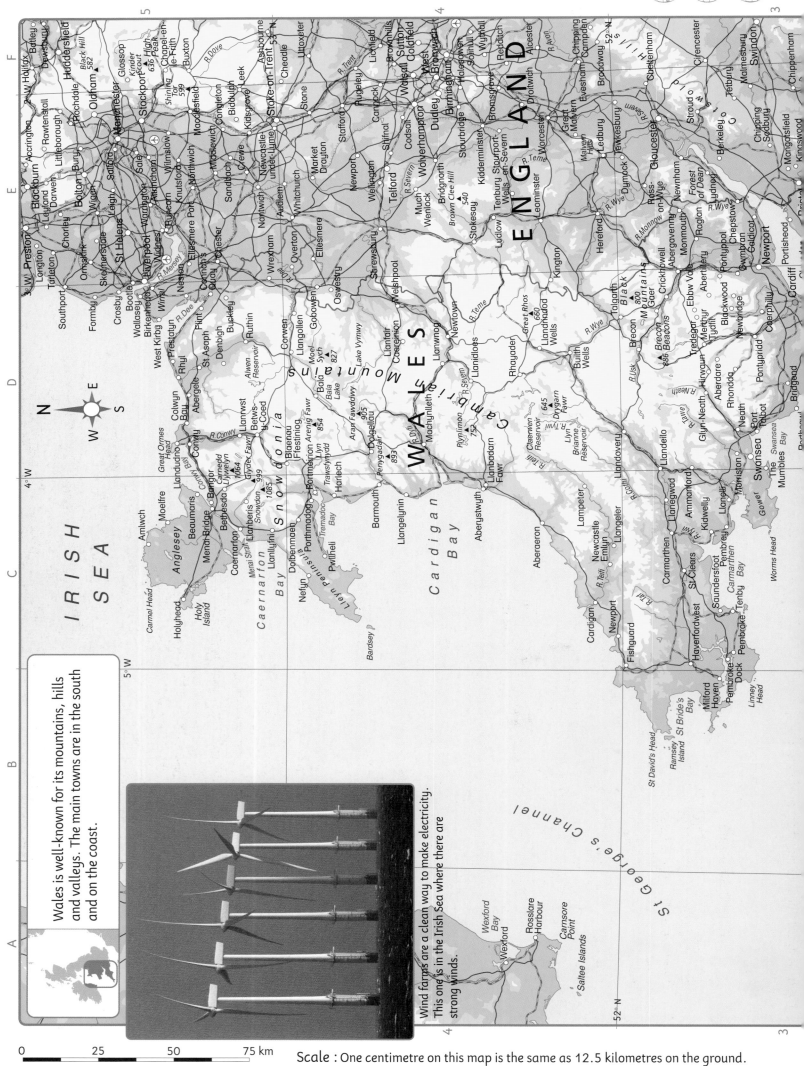

Wales is well-known for its mountains, hills and valleys. The main towns are in the south and on the coast.

Wind farms are a clean way to make electricity. This one is in the Irish Sea where there are strong winds.

Scale : One centimetre on this map is the same as 12.5 kilometres on the ground.

0   25   50   75 km

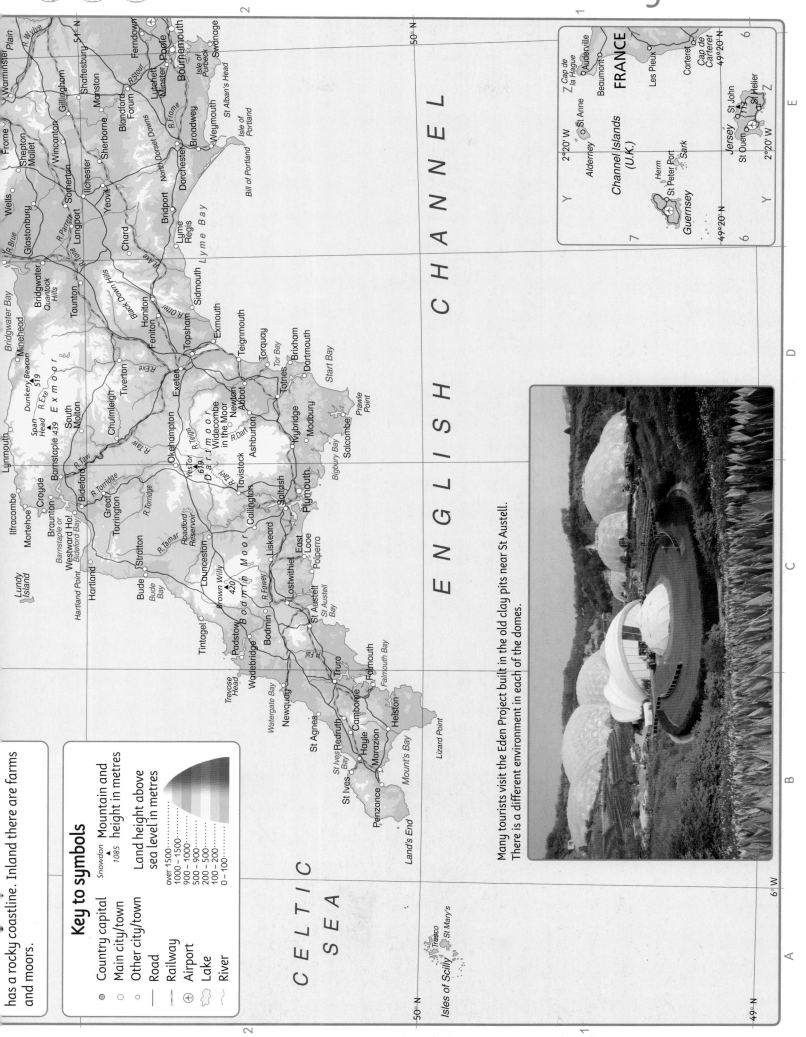

has a rocky coastline. Inland there are farms and moors.

Key to symbols

- ● Country capital
- ◉ Main city/town
- ○ Other city/town
- — Road
- ⊢ Railway
- ✈ Airport
- Lake
- River

Snowdon ▲ 1085   Mountain and height in metres

Land height above sea level in metres

- over 1500
- 1000 – 1500
- 900 – 1000
- 500 – 900
- 200 – 500
- 100 – 200
- 0 – 100

Many tourists visit the Eden Project built in the old clay pits near St Austell. There is a different environment in each of the domes.

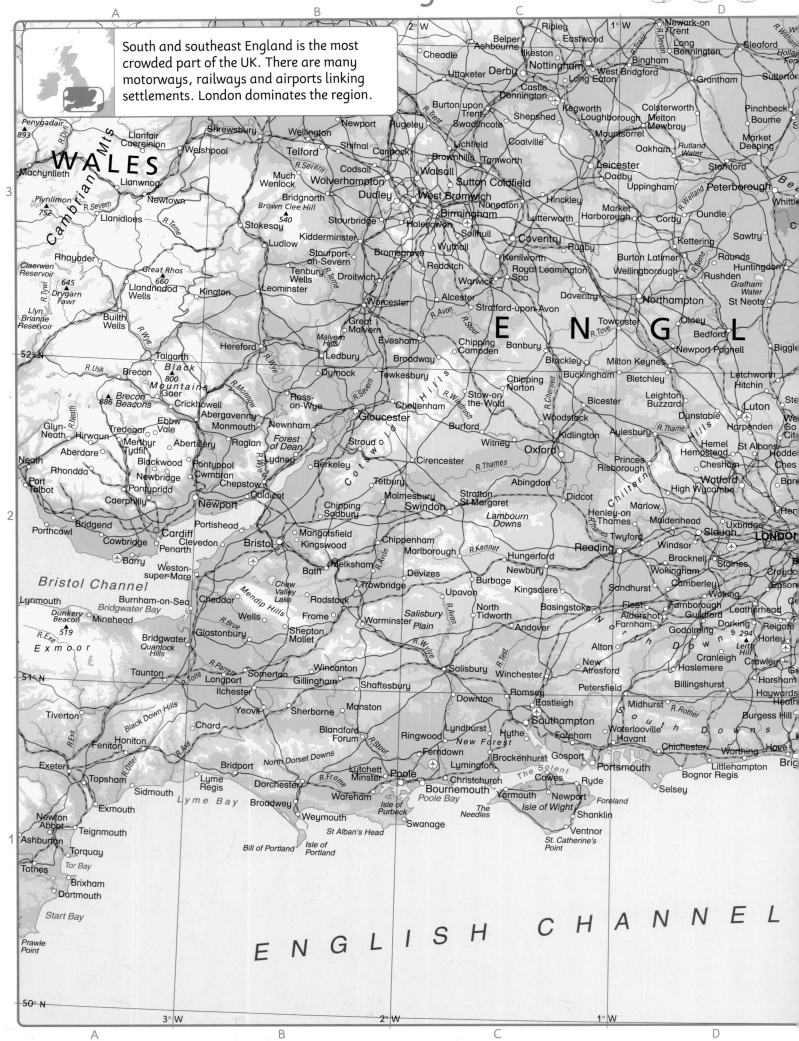

South and southeast England is the most crowded part of the UK. There are many motorways, railways and airports linking settlements. London dominates the region.

Scale : One centimetre on this map is the same as 12.5 kilometres on the ground.

0   25   50   75 km

E   F   G   H

1° E   2° E   3° E   53° N

Key to symbols

- ▪ Capital city
- ◉ Country capital
- ○ Main city/town
- ○ Other city/town
- ── Country boundary
- ── Road
- ┉ Railway
- ✈ Airport
- Lake
- River
- ▲ *Leith Hill* Mountain and
  294   height in metres

Land height above
sea level in metres

over 1500
1000 – 1500
900 – 1000
500 – 900
200 – 500
100 – 200
0 – 100

Land below
sea level

The Wash

NORTH
SEA

ngle

Hunstanton
Wells-next-the-Sea
Cromer
King's Lynn
Narborough
East Dereham
Fakenham
Aylsham
Coltishall
North Walsham
R.Wensum
Swaffham
Wymondham
Norwich
Hoveton
R. Bure
Downham Market
Great R.Ouse
sbech
ington
Southery
Mundford
R. Thet
Loddon
Norfolk Broads
Great Yarmouth
R.Yare
Littleport
Long Stratton
Corton
Lowestoft
Ely
Thetford
Scole
R.Waveney
Bungay
Kessingland
R.Cam
Soham
Little R.Ouse
R.Dove
Halesworth
wmarket bridge
Stanton
Bury St Edmunds
Haverhill
Stowmarket
Wickham Market
Saxmundham

N D

Saffron Walden
Sudbury
Claydon
Aldeburgh
Orford Ness
Newport
Capel St Mary
Ipswich
R.Colne
Halstead
R.Stour
Felixstowe
Braintree
Coggeshall
Colchester
Harwich
shop's ortford
Great Dunmow
Brightlingsea
The Naze
low
Witham
Frinton-on-Sea
Chelmsford
R.Chelmer
Clacton-on-Sea
Maldon
R.Blackwater
pping
Ingatestone
Southminster
ngar
Brentwood
R.Crouch
Foulness Point
Basildon
Rayleigh
South Ockendon
Southend-on-Sea
River Thames
Tilbury
Grain
Sheerness
Gravesend
Isle of Sheppey
Margate
North Foreland
Rochester
Gillingham
Herne Bay
Broadstairs
North
Chatham
Whitstable
Isle of Thanet
Ramsgate
Sevenoaks
Sittingbourne
Faversham
Downs
Maidstone
Chilham
Canterbury
R.Medway
Chilham
Eastry
Deal
ge
Barham
Royal Tunbridge Wells
Ashford
R.Beult
Sellindge
Dover
e
Hamstreet
Folkestone
Weald
Hawkhurst
Hythe
rowborough
Romney Marsh
Heathfield
Salehurst
New Romney
eld
Rye
Lydd
Hailsham
R.Stour
Gt. R.Stour

N

W   E

S

Oosterschelde

NETHERLANDS

Goes

Vlissingen

Westerschelde

Terneuzen

Zeebrugge

Ostend

Brugge

Scheldt

Nieuwpoort

Veurne

BELGIUM

Gent

Dunkerque

Diksmuide

Tielt

54° N

Guines

Gravelines

Roeselare

Ieper

Yser

Ijzer

Lys

Oudenaarde

Kortrijk

164
▲
Mont des Cats

Ronse

Mouscron

Roubaix

Strait of Dover

Channel Tunnel

Calais

Coulogne

F R A N C E

Wimereux

St-Omer

Hazebrouck

Boulogne

Hastings
Bexhill
Eastbourne
Beachy Head
Rye Bay
Dungeness
legate
en

52° N

3

2

1

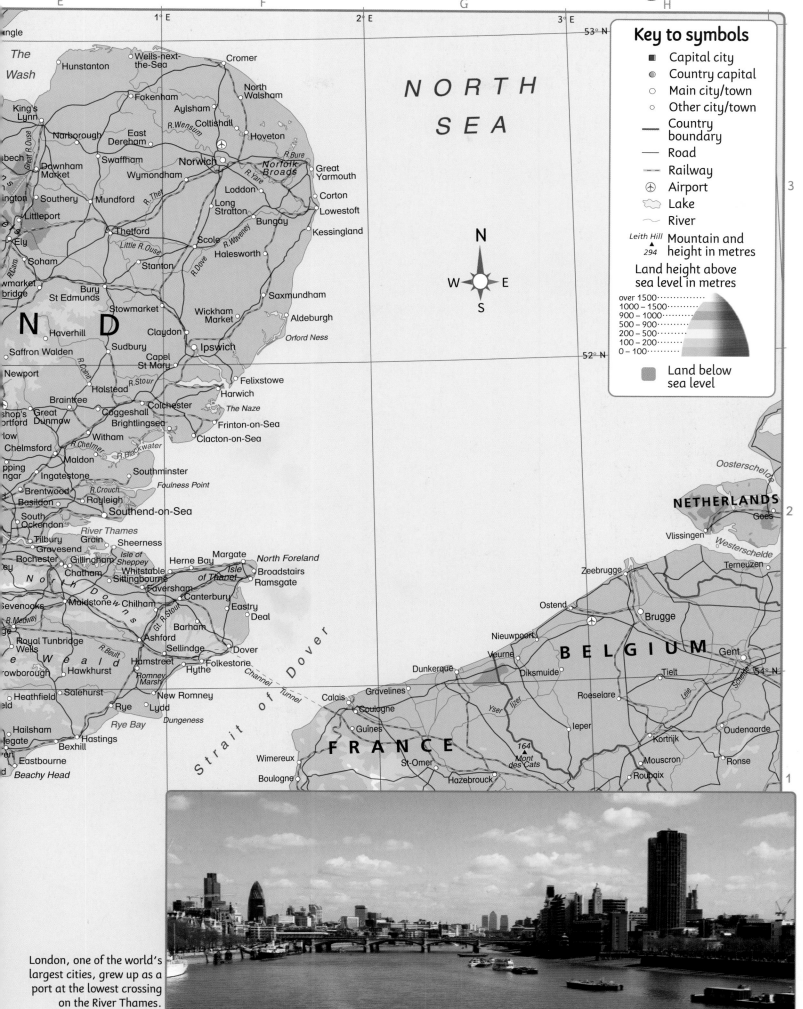

London, one of the world's largest cities, grew up as a port at the lowest crossing on the River Thames.

E

The highest mountains are in the north and west of Great Britain. The south and east are much flatter with low hills. The main rivers such as the Severn, Trent and Thames flow through these areas.

Key to symbols

Land height above sea level in metres

over 1000
500 – 1000
200 – 500
100 – 200
0 – 100

Ben Nevis ▲ 1344   Mountain and height in metres

‒‒ River

Lake

Land below sea level

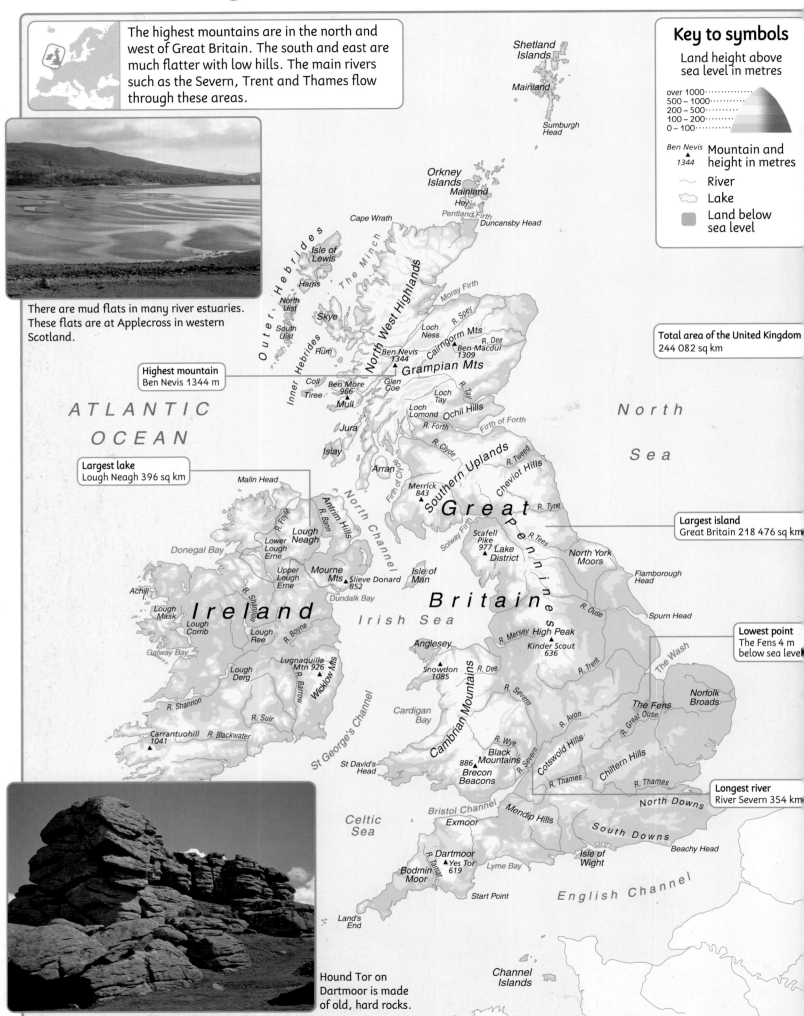

There are mud flats in many river estuaries. These flats are at Applecross in western Scotland.

Highest mountain
Ben Nevis 1344 m

Largest lake
Lough Neagh 396 sq km

Total area of the United Kingdom
244 082 sq km

Largest island
Great Britain 218 476 sq km

Lowest point
The Fens 4 m below sea level

Longest river
River Severn 354 km

Hound Tor on Dartmoor is made of old, hard rocks.

Map labels

Shetland Islands — Mainland — Sumburgh Head
Orkney Islands — Mainland — Hoy — Pentland Firth — Duncansby Head
Cape Wrath
Outer Hebrides — Isle of Lewis — Harris — North Uist — South Uist
The Minch
North West Highlands — Ben Nevis 1344 — Grampian Mts
Moray Firth — R. Spey — Cairngorm Mts — R. Dee — Ben Macdui 1309
Loch Ness
Inner Hebrides — Skye — Rum — Coll — Tiree — Mull — Ben More 966 — Glen Coe
Jura — Islay — Arran
Loch Lomond — Loch Tay — R. Tay — Ochil Hills — Firth of Forth
R. Forth — R. Clyde — Firth of Clyde
ATLANTIC OCEAN
Southern Uplands — Merrick 843 — R. Tweed — Cheviot Hills
Great Britain — Pennines
R. Tyne — R. Tees — Scafell Pike 977 — Lake District — North York Moors
Solway Firth — Flamborough Head — Spurn Head
Malin Head — Donegal Bay — R. Foyle — R. Bann — Antrim Hills — Lough Neagh
Lower Lough Erne — Upper Lough Erne — Mourne Mts — Slieve Donard 852 — Dundalk Bay
North Channel — Isle of Man
Achill I. — Lough Mask — Lough Corrib — R. Shannon — Lough Ree — Lough Derg
Ireland — R. Boyne — R. Barrow — Lugnaquilla Mtn 926 — Wicklow Mts
Galway Bay — R. Shannon — R. Suir — Carrantuohill 1041 — R. Blackwater
Irish Sea — Anglesey — R. Dee — Snowdon 1085 — High Peak — Kinder Scout 636
R. Mersey — R. Ouse — R. Trent — The Wash — Norfolk Broads
Cambrian Mountains — R. Severn — R. Avon — The Fens — R. Great Ouse
Cardigan Bay — St George's Channel — St David's Head
Black Mountains 886 — Brecon Beacons — R. Wye — R. Severn — Cotswold Hills — Chiltern Hills
R. Thames — R. Thames — North Downs
Bristol Channel — Mendip Hills — South Downs — Beachy Head
Celtic Sea — Exmoor — Dartmoor — Yes Tor 619 — Bodmin Moor
Lyme Bay — Isle of Wight — R. ... — Start Point — Land's End
English Channel — Channel Islands
North Sea

0   50   100   150   200   250 km

Scale : One centimetre on this map is the same as 50 kilometres on the ground.

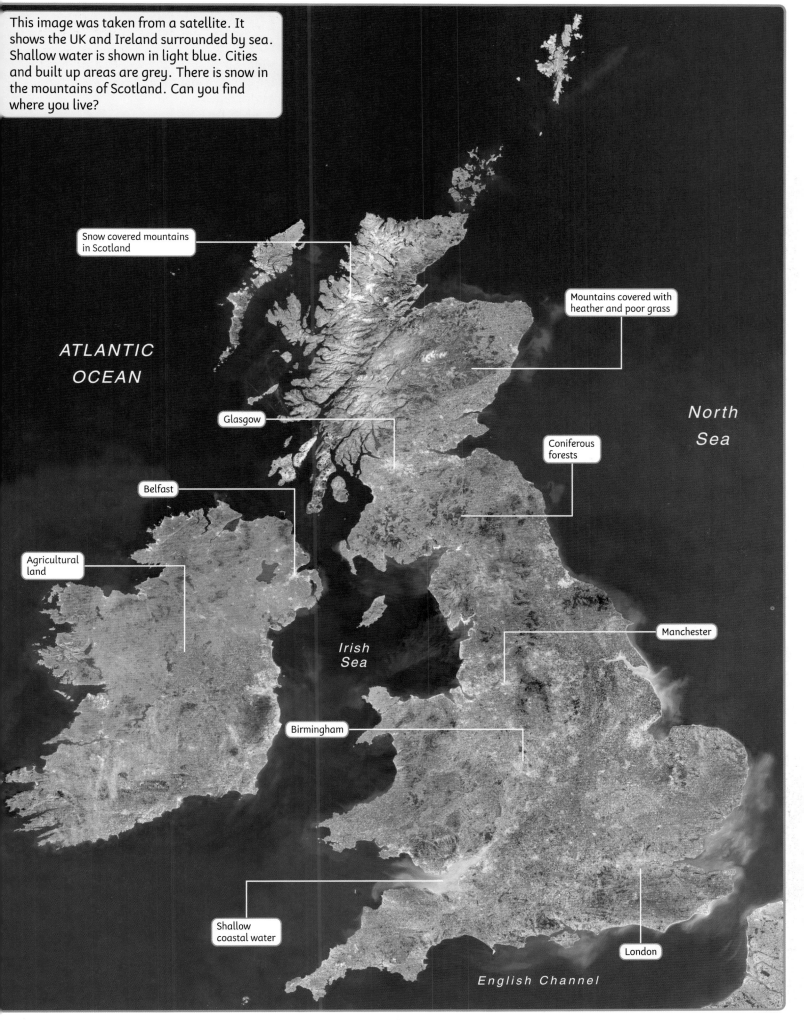

This image was taken from a satellite. It shows the UK and Ireland surrounded by sea. Shallow water is shown in light blue. Cities and built up areas are grey. There is snow in the mountains of Scotland. Can you find where you live?

Snow covered mountains in Scotland

Mountains covered with heather and poor grass

ATLANTIC OCEAN

North Sea

Glasgow

Coniferous forests

Belfast

Agricultural land

Manchester

Irish Sea

Birmingham

Shallow coastal water

London

English Channel

The mixture of sun, rain and wind make the weather.

Extreme weather causes problems. In July 2007 torrential rain flooded Tewkesbury and other parts of central England.

Annual rainfall

All parts of the UK have rain throughout the year. Western areas are the wettest. Here winds from the sea shed water as they rise over the mountains.

Average annual rainfall
- more than 2000 mm
- 1500 – 2000 mm
- 1000 – 1500 mm
- 750 – 1000 mm
- 625 – 750 mm
- less than 625 mm
- Location of places on climate graphs

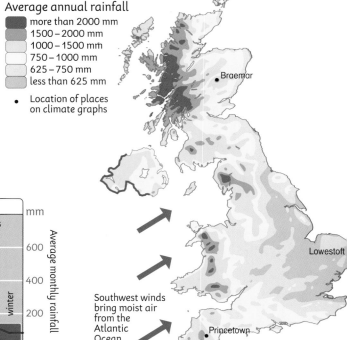

Southwest winds bring moist air from the Atlantic Ocean

Seasonal climate graphs

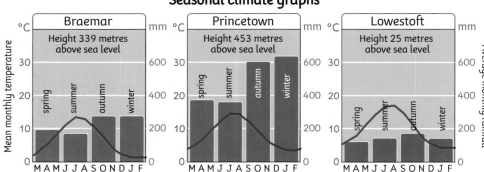

Braemar
Height 339 metres above sea level
spring summer autumn winter

Princetown
Height 453 metres above sea level
spring summer autumn winter

Lowestoft
Height 25 metres above sea level
spring summer autumn winter

Winter temperatures

In January, warm ocean currents bring milder conditions to the southwest of the UK. The coldest areas are the mountains in the north.

Average temperature
- over 6°C
- 4 – 6°C
- 2 – 4°C
- 0 – 2°C
- below 0°C
- Location of places on climate graphs

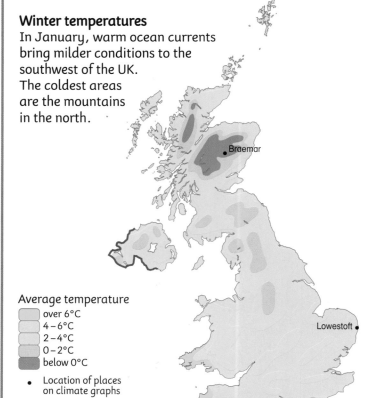

Summer temperatures

In July, the warmest parts of the UK are in the south, especially along the coasts. Mountain areas are the coolest.

Average temperature
- over 16°C
- 14 – 16°C
- 12 – 14°C
- 10 – 12°C
- below 10°C
- Location of places on climate graphs

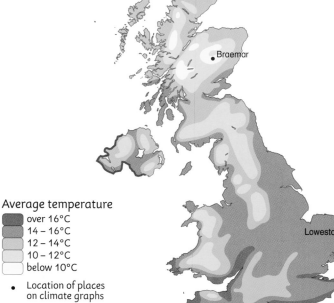

Country populations

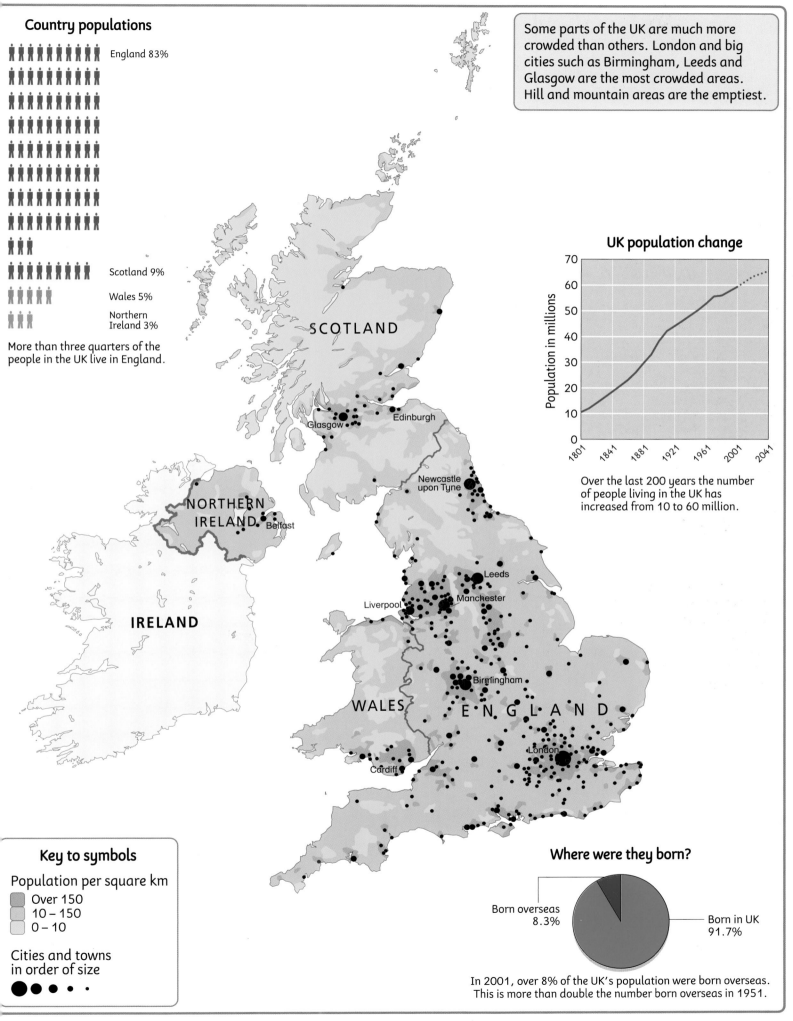

England 83%

Scotland 9%

Wales 5%

Northern Ireland 3%

More than three quarters of the people in the UK live in England.

Some parts of the UK are much more crowded than others. London and big cities such as Birmingham, Leeds and Glasgow are the most crowded areas. Hill and mountain areas are the emptiest.

UK population change

Population in millions

70
60
50
40
30
20
10
0

1801 1841 1881 1921 1961 2001 2041

Over the last 200 years the number of people living in the UK has increased from 10 to 60 million.

SCOTLAND

Glasgow Edinburgh

NORTHERN IRELAND Belfast

IRELAND

Newcastle upon Tyne

Leeds

Liverpool Manchester

Birmingham

WALES E N G L A N D

Cardiff London

Where were they born?

Born overseas 8.3%

Born in UK 91.7%

In 2001, over 8% of the UK's population were born overseas. This is more than double the number born overseas in 1951.

Key to symbols

Population per square km

Over 150
10 – 150
0 – 10

Cities and towns in order of size

50 100 150 200 250 km

Scale : One centimetre on this map is the same as 50 kilometres on the ground.

Roads and railways link the main cities in the UK. There are ferry services to mainland Europe, Ireland and other islands. Some places also have airports. How many can you find on the map?

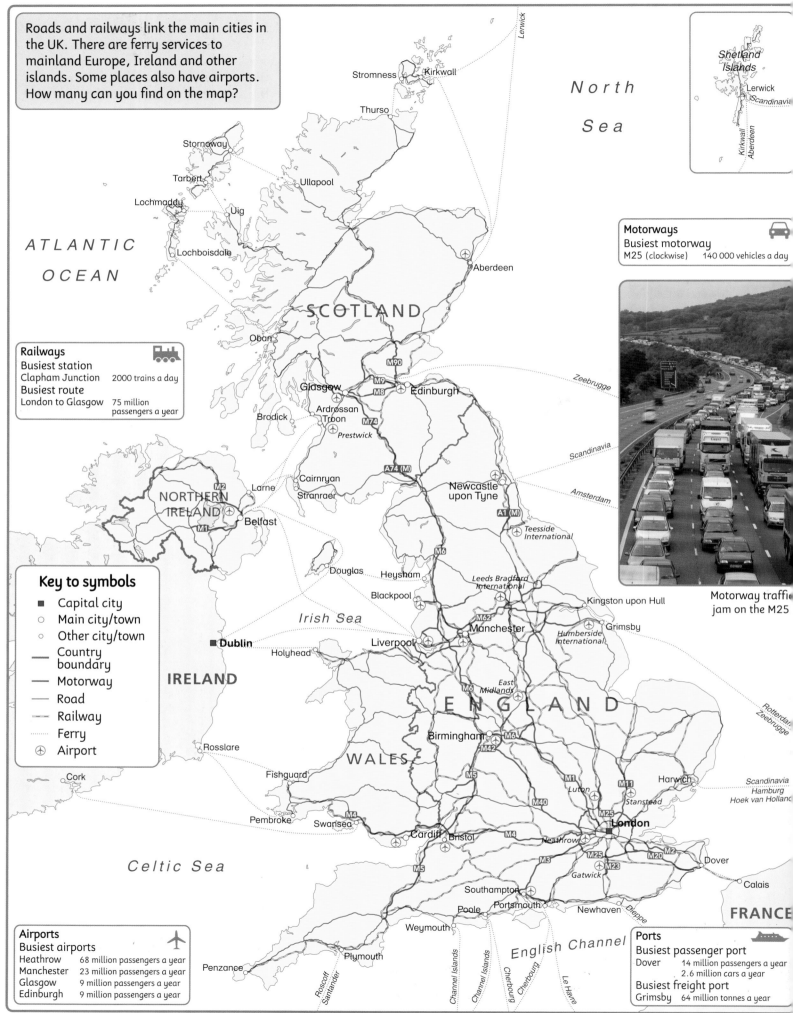

Motorways
Busiest motorway
M25 (clockwise)   140 000 vehicles a day

Motorway traffic jam on the M25

Railways
Busiest station
Clapham Junction   2000 trains a day
Busiest route
London to Glasgow   75 million passengers a year

Key to symbols
- ■ Capital city
- ○ Main city/town
- ○ Other city/town
- ━ Country boundary
- ━ Motorway
- ━ Road
- ┿ Railway
- ⋯ Ferry
- ✈ Airport

Airports
Busiest airports
Heathrow   68 million passengers a year
Manchester   23 million passengers a year
Glasgow   9 million passengers a year
Edinburgh   9 million passengers a year

Ports
Busiest passenger port
Dover   14 million passengers a year
         2.6 million cars a year
Busiest freight port
Grimsby   64 million tonnes a year

North Sea
Atlantic Ocean
Irish Sea
Celtic Sea
English Channel

Shetland Islands
Lerwick
Kirkwall
Aberdeen

SCOTLAND
Stromness Kirkwall
Thurso
Stornoway
Tarbert
Ullapool
Lochmaddy
Uig
Lochboisdale
Oban
Brodick
Glasgow Edinburgh
Ardrossan Troon Prestwick
M90 M9 M8 M74

NORTHERN IRELAND
M2 M1
Belfast
Larne
Cairnryan
Stranraer
A74 (M)

Newcastle upon Tyne
A1 (M)
Teesside International
M6

Douglas Heysham
Blackpool
Leeds Bradford International
Kingston upon Hull
Manchester
Liverpool
M62
Grimsby
Humberside International
Holyhead
■ Dublin
IRELAND
Rosslare
Fishguard
Pembroke
Swansea
M4
Cardiff Bristol
M5
WALES
ENGLAND
East Midlands
Birmingham M6
M42
M5
M1 M11 Harwich
Luton Stanstead
M40
London ■
M25 M2
Heathrow
M4
M3 M23 M20 Dover
Gatwick Calais
Southampton
Poole Portsmouth
Weymouth Newhaven Dieppe
Plymouth
Penzance

FRANCE

Zeebrugge
Scandinavia
Amsterdam
Rotterdam Zeebrugge
Scandinavia Hamburg Hoek van Holland
Cork
Roscoff Santander
Channel Islands Channel Islands
Cherbourg Cherbourg Le Havre

The European Union (EU) was set up in 1957 to keep peace between nations and improve people's lives. Since then it has grown larger and more powerful. It now has 27 member states with others waiting to join.

ICELAND

NORWAY
SWEDEN
FINLAND
ESTONIA
LATVIA
LITHUANIA
8
DENMARK
UNITED KINGDOM
IRELAND
NETHERLANDS
BELARUS
Brussels
BELGIUM
GERMANY
POLAND
1
CZECH REPUBLIC
UKRAINE
Strasbourg
SLOVAKIA
2
AUSTRIA
HUNGARY
7
FRANCE
3
CROATIA
ROMANIA
4
SERBIA
5
BULGARIA
6
ITALY
ALBANIA
PORTUGAL
SPAIN
TURKEY
GREECE
MALTA
CYPRUS

Key to symbols

- ■ Founder member in 1957
- ■ Joined 1957-2007
- □ Hoping to join
- □ Other countries

1 LUXEMBOURG
2 SWITZERLAND
3 SLOVENIA
4 BOSNIA-HERZEGOVINA
5 MONTENEGRO
6 MACEDONIA
7 MOLDOVA
8 RUSSIAN FEDERATION

The EU flag.

The European Union

The European Union was founded in 1957.
The timeline shows when each country joined it.

	1957		**1973**	**1981**	**1986**	**1995**	**2004**	**2007**
Belgium Germany France Italy Luxembourg Netherlands			Denmark Ireland UK	Greece	Spain Portugal	Austria Finland Sweden	Cyprus Czech Republic Estonia Hungary Latvia Lithuania Malta Poland Slovakia Slovenia	Bulgaria Romania
Population of the EU	167 million		257 million	271 million	367 million	373 million	456 million	494 million

50   1960   1970   1980   1990   2000   2010

European laws are made in the parliament which meets in Brussels and Strasbourg. This photograph shows the Government Building of the European Union in Strasbourg.

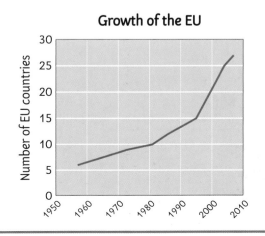

Growth of the EU

Number of EU countries

30
25
20
15
10
5
0

1950 1960 1970 1980 1990 2000 2010

There are over 40 countries in Europe.
Ukraine and France are the largest.
Malta and Andorra are two of the smallest.

ARCTIC OCEAN

Novaya Zemlya

Total population of Europe
(excluding Russian Federation)
589 million

Russian Federation
Area 17 million sq km
Population 143 million

Jan Mayen
(Norway)

ICELAND
■ Reykjavík

Country with most people
(excluding Russian Federation)
Germany 83 million

White Sea

RUSSIAN

FEDERATION

ATLANTIC

OCEAN

Faroe Islands
(Denmark)

N O R W A Y
S W E D E N
F I N L A N D
Gulf of Bothnia

Helsinki ■
○ St Petersburg

Largest city
Moscow 11 million

Oslo ■
Stockholm ■

Tallinn ■
ESTONIA

■ Moscow

Edinburgh ○ *North Sea*

LATVIA
Riga ■

Belfast ○
Dublin ■
IRELAND
UNITED
KINGDOM

DENMARK
Copenhagen ■

Baltic Sea

LITHUANIA
Vilnius ■
Minsk ■

○ Volgograd

Berlin ■

Warsaw ■
POLAND

BELARUS

London ■

2
GERMANY
1
3

Prague ■
CZECH REPUBLIC

Kiev ■
UKRAINE

Caspian Sea

English Channel

Largest city
(Western Europe)
Paris 10 million

■ Paris

Munich ○
Vienna ■
7
Bratislava ■
AUSTRIA
Budapest ■
HUNGARY

MOLDOVA
Chişinău ■
Odesa ○

FRANCE

Bay of Biscay

Lyon ○
Milan ○

4

5
CROATIA
Zagreb ■
6
ROMANIA
Belgrade ■
SERBIA
Bucharest ■

Black Sea

Largest country
(excluding Russian Federation)
Ukraine 603 700 sq km

PORTUGAL
Madrid ■
Barcelona ○

Corsica

SAN MARINO
Adriatic Sea

8
Skopje ■
10
Sofia ■
BULGARIA

Istanbul ○
TURKEY

A S I A

Lisbon ■
SPAIN

Balearic Islands
Palma de Mallorca ○

ITALY
Rome ■
Tirana ■
ALBANIA

TURKEY

Strait of Gibraltar
Gibraltar (UK) ○

ANDORRA

Sardinia

Sicily

GREECE
Aegean Sea

Athens ■

Mediterranean Sea

Crete
Rhodes

MALTA

1 BELGIUM
2 NETHERLANDS
3 LUXEMBOURG
4 SWITZERLAND
5 SLOVENIA
6 BOSNIA-HERZEGOVINA
7 SLOVAKIA
8 MONTENEGRO
9 RUSSIAN FEDERATION
10 MACEDONIA

A F R I C A

Key to symbols

◢ Countries
■ Capital city
○ Important city/town

Ancient buildings around
Red Square, Moscow.

Scale : One centimetre on this map is the same as 250 kilometres on the ground.

Europe, one of the smallest continents, has a very long coast. The North European Plain is a large lowland area. The Alps and Caucasus are the highest mountain ranges.

Total area of Europe
10 million sq km

Largest lake completely in Europe
Lake Ladoga 18 390 sq km

Largest island
Great Britain 218 476 sq km

Lowest point
Caspian Sea shore 28 metres below sea level

Longest river
Volga 3688 km

Largest lake (Europe/Asia)
Caspian Sea 371 000 sq km

Highest mountain
El'brus 5642 m

ARCTIC OCEAN

ATLANTIC OCEAN

ASIA

AFRICA

Greenland

Spitsbergen

Novaya Zemlya

Jan Mayen

Iceland

Faroe Islands

Shetland Islands

Orkney Islands

British Isles

Ireland

Great Britain

North Sea

Lofoten Is

North Cape

Kola Peninsula

White Sea

Lappland

Scandinavia

Gulf of Bothnia

Lake Onega

Lake Ladoga

Lake Peipus

Vänern

Vättern

Jutland

Baltic Sea

North European Plain

R. Dvina

R. Pechora

R. Northern Dvina

R. Sukhona

R. Volga

Ural Mountains

Volga Uplands

Central Russian Uplands

Caspian Lowland

R. Thames

English Channel

R. Seine

R. Loire

R. Rhine

R. Elbe

R. Oder

R. Vistula

Sudeten Mts

R. Dniester

R. Dnieper

R. Don

R. Donets

R. Don

R. Volga

Bay of Biscay

Cape Finisterre

Cantabrian Mts

R. Duero

R. Ebro

Pyrenees
3404

Iberian Peninsula

R. Tagus

Sierra Nevada

Cape Vincent

Strait of Gibraltar

Jura

Massif Central

Mont Blanc
4808

Alps

R. Rhône

R. Po

Corsica

Balearic Islands

Sardinia

Apennines

Dinaric Alps

Adriatic Sea

Carpathian Mountains

Hungarian Plain

R. Danube

Balkan Mts

Pindus Mts

Aegean Sea

Crete

Rhodes

Black Sea

Caucasus

El'brus
5642

Caspian Sea

ASIA

Mediterranean Sea

Malta

Mount Etna
Sicily
3323

Key to symbols

Land height above sea level in metres

- over 5000
- 2000 – 5000
- 1000 – 2000
- 500 – 1000
- 200 – 500
- 0 – 200

El'brus
5642 Mountain and height in metres

River

Lake

Seasonal lake

Ice cap

Land below sea level

Mount Etna is one of the world's most active volcanoes. Its last major eruption was in 2002.

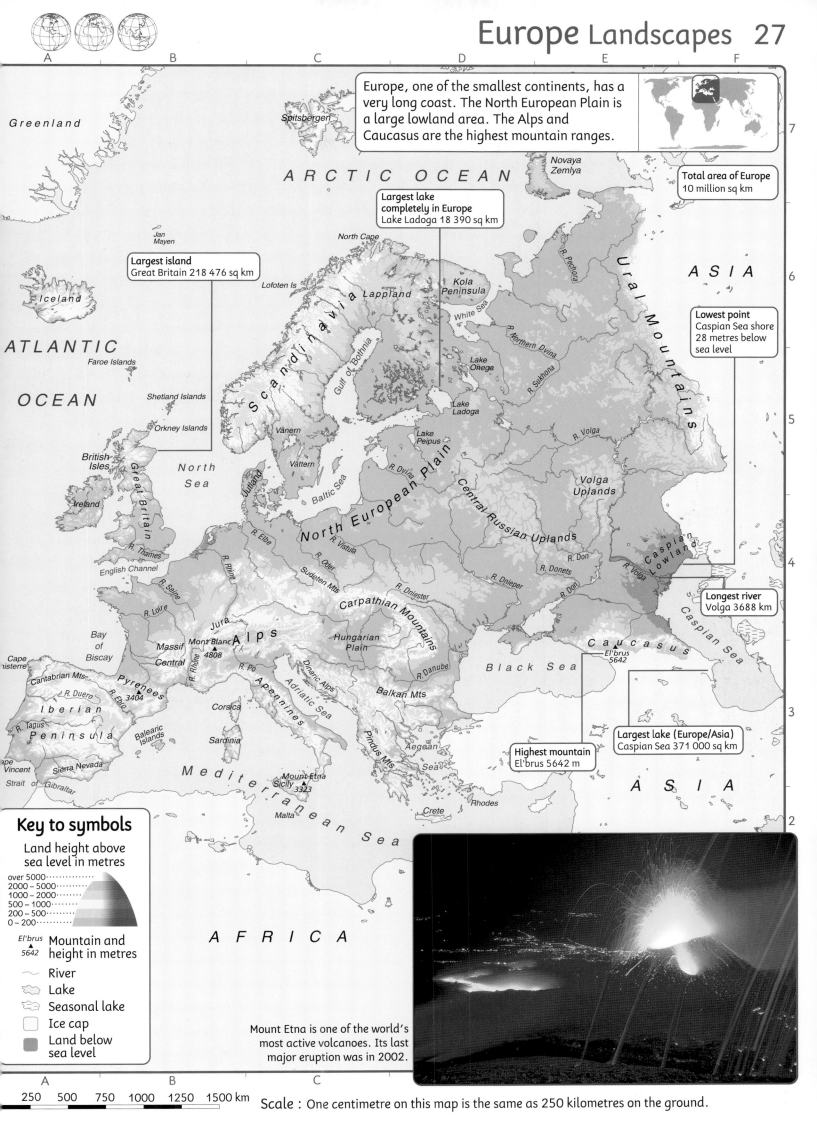

A	B	C
250	500	750

250   500   750   1000   1250   1500 km

Scale : One centimetre on this map is the same as 250 kilometres on the ground.

Three Scandinavian countries – Norway, Sweden and Denmark – lie at the heart of northern Europe. They have similar traditions and beliefs. In the past, the people who lived there also all spoke the same language.

ICELAND

Akureyri

Arctic Circle

Reykjavik

Vatnajökull

Seyðhisfjörðhur

Tromsø

Lofoten Islands

Narvik

Bodø

N O R W E G I A N

S E A

Norwegian Sea

60° N

Faroe Islands (Denmark)

Trondheim

Östersund

Ålesund

Sundsvall

Galdhøpiggen 2470

Lillehammer

Umeå

Shetland Islands

Bergen

Uppsala

A T L A N T I C

O C E A N

Outer Hebrides

Orkney Islands

Inverness

Ben Nevis 1344

Grampian Mountains

Aberdeen

Stavanger

Drammen

Oslo

Karlstad

Örebro

Västerås

Stock

Norrköping

Kristiansand

Vänern

55° N

Glasgow

Edinburgh

Dundee

N o r t h
S e a

Gothenburg

Vättern

Jönköping

Götland

Skagerrak

Aalborg

Kattegat

DENMARK

Halmstad

Öland

Londonderry

Carlisle

Newcastle upon Tyne

Århus

Karlskrona

Belfast

UNITED

Copenhagen

Galway

IRELAND

KINGDOM

Esbjerg

Odense

Malmö

B a l t i c

Limerick

Blackpool

Irish Sea

Liverpool

Leeds

Manchester

Dublin

Bornholm

Cork

Wexford

Sheffield

Kiel

Gdańsk

Koszalin

Birmingham

Nottingham

Rostock

Groningen

Hamburg

Szczecin

Swansea

Norwich

NETHERLANDS

R. Elbe

Bremen

Bydgoszcz

Cardiff

Oxford

Amsterdam

IJsselmeer

Hannover

R. Oder

Poznań

Bristol

R. Thames

The Hague

R. Weser

Berlin

London

Rotterdam

Duisburg

Magdeburg

POLA

Dover

Eindhoven

GERMANY

Zielona Góra

Plymouth

Southampton

Brugge

Antwerp

Dortmund

Essen

Leipzig

Dresden

R. Oder

Wrocław

Strait of Dover

Calais

Lille

BELGIUM

Brussels

Düsseldorf

Cologne

Bonn

Erfurt

Ka

English Channel

Liège

Sudeten Mts

Channel Islands

Le Havre

Amiens

LUXEMBOURG

Frankfurt

Prague

Brest

Rouen

Luxembourg

Mainz

CZECH

Ostrava

Rennes

Caen

R. Seine

Reims

Nuremberg

Plzeň

REPUBLIC

Brno

Paris

Nancy

Karlsruhe

SL

Le Mans

Orléans

R. Seine

Strasbourg

Stuttgart

R. Danube

Vienna

Nantes

R. Loire

FRANCE

R. Loire

R. Rhine

R. Inn

Linz

Bratisl

Tours

Munich

Salzburg

Budape

La Rochelle

Poitiers

Dijon

Basel

Zürich

Innsbruck

AUSTRIA

Graz

HU

Bern

SWITZERLAND

LIECHTENSTEIN

ICELAND, SWEDEN, NORWAY, FINLAND labels along right edge

L M N O P Q R

30° E   35° E   40° E   45° E   50° E   55° E

Barents Sea

Kirkenes

Murmansk

Kola Peninsula

Mezen'

R. Pechora

Ukhta

Arctic Circle

65° N

6

Kandalaksha

White Sea

Archangel

Severodvinsk

Syktyvkar

5

Oulu

Belomorsk

R. Northern Dvina

Kotlas

60° N

FINLAND

Kuopio

Medvezh'yegorsk

Lake Onega

Petrozavodsk

Konosha

R. Sukhona

Jyväskylä

Tampere

Lahti

Lake Ladoga

RUSSIAN

Vologda

4

Vantaa

Helsinki

St Petersburg

Cherepovets

Rybinsk Reservoir

R. Volga

Kostroma

Gulf of Finland

Tallinn

Lake Peipus

Velikiy Novgorod

Rybinsk

Yaroslavl'

Ivanovo

ESTONIA

Pärnu

Tartu

FEDERATION

Nizhniy Novgorod

Gulf of Riga

Pskov

Tver'

Vladimir

55° N

LATVIA

Velikiye Luki

Saransk

Riga

R. Dvina

Šiauliai

Daugavpils

Vitsyebsk

Smolensk

Kaluga

Tula

Ryazan'

LITHUANIA

Orsha

Tambov

FED.

Kaunas

Vilnius

Mahilyow

Bryansk

Orel

Lipetsk

50° N

Minsk

Balashov

Hrodna

Babruysk

R. Dnieper

Kursk

Voronezh

Borisoglebsk

BELARUS

Baranavichy

Homyel'

R. Don

Białystok

Brest

Mazyr

Chernihiv

Sumy

Belgorod

Warsaw

Lublin

Rivne

Kiev

Zhytomyr

UKRAINE

L'vov

Khmel'nyts'kyy

Košice

Chernivtsi

R. Dniester

Vinnytsya

Carpathian Mountains

Satu Mare

Pietrosa 2305

MOLDOVA

Chişinău

ROMANIA

Cluj-Napoca

Bacău

Bălţi

25° E

K L M N

Iceland is famous for hot springs and geysers. As well as attracting tourists, geysers are a valuable source of power.

Key to symbols

■ Capital city	☐ Ice cap
○ Main city/town	*Galdhøpiggen* ▲ **2470** Mountain and height in metres
◦ Other city/town	Land height above sea level in metres
—— Country boundary	over 5000
—— Road	3000 – 5000
—— Railway	2000 – 3000
～ Canal	1000 – 2000
⊕ Airport	500 – 1000
Lake	200 – 500
River	0 – 200
	Land below sea level

Capital populations

Bar chart showing capital populations in Millions:
- London: ~8.6
- Paris: ~9.8
- Brussels: ~1.1
- Oslo: ~0.9
- Berlin: ~3.4
- Prague: ~1.2
- Moscow: ~11.0

The Mediterranean Sea links many of the countries of southern Europe. In the past, the Romans and Ancient Greeks both had empires here. Today, good summer weather makes the Mediterranean popular for holidays.

Cross section through the Alps

Scale : One centimetre on this map is the same as 100 kilometres on the ground

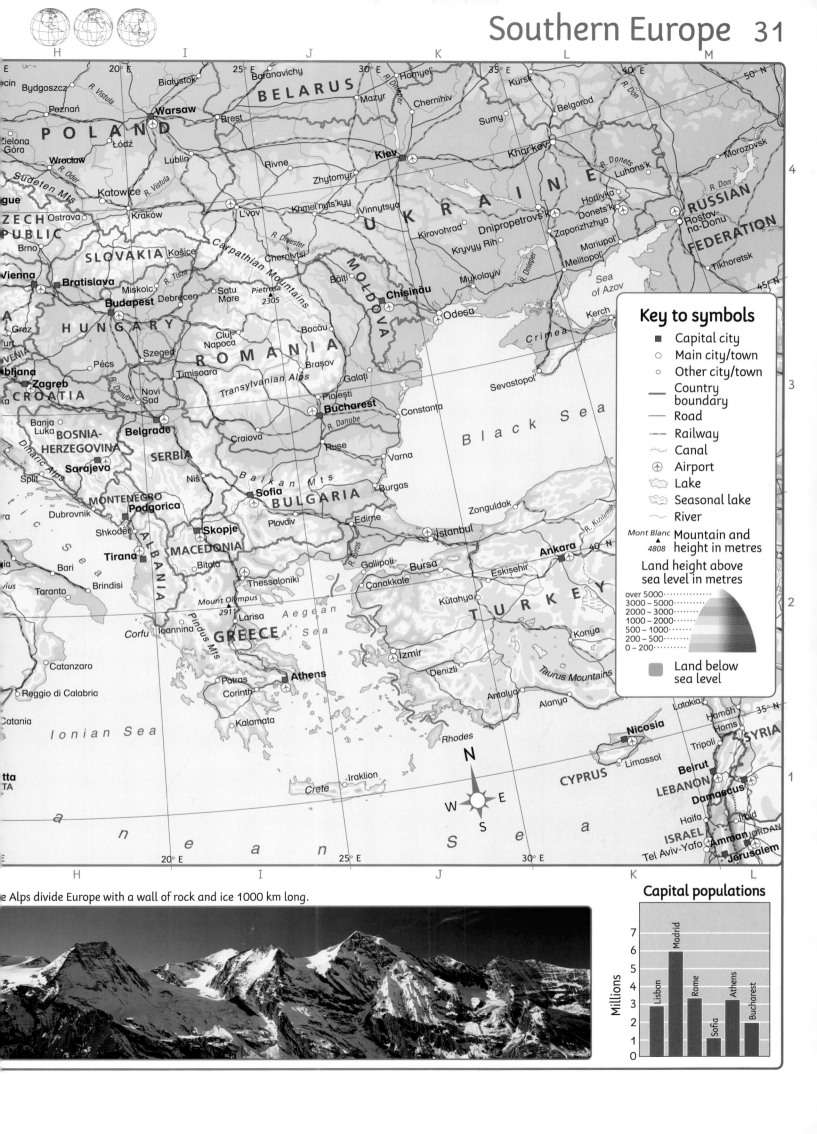

Key to symbols

- ■ Capital city
- ○ Main city/town
- ○ Other city/town
- —— Country boundary
- —— Road
- —— Railway
- ⌁ Canal
- ⊕ Airport
- Lake
- Seasonal lake
- River
- ▲ *Mont Blanc* **4808** Mountain and height in metres

Land height above sea level in metres

- over 5000
- 3000 – 5000
- 2000 – 3000
- 1000 – 2000
- 500 – 1000
- 200 – 500
- 0 – 200

Land below sea level

The Alps divide Europe with a wall of rock and ice 1000 km long.

Capital populations

Lisbon, Madrid, Sofia, Rome, Athens, Bucharest

There are 54 countries in Africa. The largest, Sudan, has fewer people than the UK but is ten times the size. Some African countries have no sea coast. How many can you find?

Key to symbols
- Countries
- ■ Capital city
- ○ Important city/town

Country with most people
Nigeria 148 million

Total population of Africa
965 million

1 THE GAMBIA
2 GUINEA-BISSAU
3 TOGO
4 EQUATORIAL GUINEA
5 SÃO TOMÉ & PRINCIPE
6 RWANDA
7 BURUNDI

EUROPE

Azores (Portugal)

Mediterranean Sea

Algiers
Tunis
TUNISIA
Tripoli

Benghazi

Alexandria
Giza Cairo

A S I A

Madeira (Portugal)
Casablanca
Rabat
MOROCCO

Canary Is (Spain)

Laayoune
WESTERN SAHARA

A L G E R I A

L I B Y A

EGYPT

Largest country
Sudan 3 million sq km

Red Sea

MAURITANIA

CAPE VERDE

Nouakchott

M A L I

NIGER

CHAD

Khartoum
Asmara
ERITREA

DJIBOUTI
Djibouti

S U D A N

Praia
Dakar
SENEGAL

Bamako
BURKINA
Niamey
Ouagadougou

Lake Chad
Ndjamena

GUINEA
Conakry
Freetown
SIERRA LEONE
CÔTE D'IVOIRE
GHANA
BENIN
Porto-Novo

N I G E R I A
Abuja

CENTRAL AFRICAN REPUBLIC

Addis Ababa

ETHIOPIA

SOMALIA

Monrovia
LIBERIA
Yamoussoukro
Abidjan
Accra

Lagos

Largest city
Lagos 14 million

CAMEROON
Bangui
Yaoundé

Libreville
GABON
CONGO

DEMOCRATIC REPUBLIC OF THE CONGO

UGANDA
Kampala
Lake Turkana

KENYA
Nairobi

Mogadishu

ATLANTIC OCEAN

Brazzaville
Kinshasa

Lake Victoria

Lake Tanganyika

Dodoma
TANZANIA

Mombasa

INDIAN OCEAN

SEYCHELLES
Victoria

Ascension Island (UK)

Luanda

Dar es Salaam

Aldabra Is (Seychelles)

St Helena (UK)

ANGOLA

Lilongwe
MALAWI
Lake Nyasa

Maroni
COMOROS

Mayotte (France)

There are busy streets and markets in many African towns.

ZAMBIA
Lusaka

Harare

MOZAMBIQUE

MADAGASCAR
Antananarivo

MAURITIUS
Reunion (France)
Port Louis

NAMIBIA
Windhoek
ZIMBABWE
Beira

Walvis Bay

BOTSWANA
Gaborone
Pretoria (Tshwane)
Maputo
SWAZILAND

Johannesburg

REPUBLIC OF
Bloemfontein
LESOTHO

SOUTH AFRICA

Cape Town

The pyramids at Giza, Egypt, were buil by the pharaohs 2000 years before Christ

0 450 900 1350 1800 2250 2700 km

Scale : One centimetre on this map is the same as 450 kilometres on the ground.

Africa lies across the Equator. The Sahara desert stretches across the north. At the Equator there are rainforests. Grasslands and mountains are found in the south and east.

EUROPE

ASIA

Total area of Africa
30 million sq km

Longest river
River Nile 6695 km

Lowest point
Lake Assal
156 metres below sea level

Largest lake
Lake Victoria 68 800 sq km

Largest island
Madagascar 587 040 sq km

Azores

Madeira

Canary Islands

Cape Verde Islands

Mediterranean Sea

Atlas Mountains

Sahara

Hoggar
2918 ▲

Tibesti
3415 ▲

Qattara Depression

Libyan Desert

Sinai

R. Nile

Lake Nasser

Red Sea

R. Sénégal

R. Niger

R. Niger

Lake Chad

R. Benue

Lake Volta

Bioco

São Tomé

Gulf of Guinea

Ras Dejen
4533 ▲

Lake Tana

Ethiopian Highlands

Lake Assal

Gulf of Aden

R. White Nile

R. Blue Nile

Webi Shabeelle

INDIAN OCEAN

R. Ubangi

R. Congo

R. Congo

R. Congo

Congo Basin

Margherita Peak
5110 ▲

Mount Kenya
5199 ▲

Lake Victoria

Kilimanjaro
5892 ▲

Lake Turkana

Great Rift Valley

Lake Tanganyika

ATLANTIC OCEAN

St Helena

Bie Plateau

Lake Nyasa

R. Zambezi

R. Zambezi

Aldabra Islands

Comoro Islands

Mayotte

Madagascar

Mozambique Channel

Mauritius

Reunion

Namib Desert

Okavango Delta

Victoria Falls

R. Limpopo

Kalahari Desert

R. Orange

R. Vaal

Drakensberg

Cape of Good Hope

Key to symbols

Land height above sea level in metres

over 5000
2000 – 5000
1000 – 2000
500 – 1000
200 – 500
0 – 200

Kilimanjaro
5892 ▲ Mountain and height in metres

River

Lake

Land below sea level

The Victoria Falls on the River Zambezi are nearly two kilometres wide and form the longest curtain of water in the world.

A Bedouin nomad in the Sahara Desert with his camels.

450   900   1350   1800   2250   2700 km

Scale : One centimetre on this map is the same as 450 kilometres on the ground.

Egypt is one of the oldest countries in the world. Today it has a population of 75 million. Most people live in the valley of the River Nile. The capital, Cairo, is larger than London.

Facts about Egypt

Area......................1 million sq km
Highest Peak... Jabal Katrina 2637 m
Longest river............. Nile 6695 km
Largest lake.....L. Nasser 5248 sq km
Population...................75 million
Largest city...........Cairo 12 million

Mediterranean Sea

SYRIA

JORDAN

Haifa
Sea of Galilee
Irbid
Tel Aviv-Yafo
WEST BANK
Amman
Jerusalem
Dead Sea
GAZA
Beersheba
ISRAEL
Negev

Umm Sa'ad
Marsa Matruh
Libyan Plateau
Qattara Depression
Alexandria
Dumyat
Damanhur
Port Said
Tanta
Al Isma'iliyah
Suez Canal
Giza
Cairo
Suez
Al Jaghbub
Siwah
Al Fayyum
Bani Suwayf
Eilat
Aqaba
Sinai
Jabal Katrina 2637

Great Sand Sea

LIBYA

Al Bawiti
Bahariya Oasis
Al Minya
R. Nile
Eastern Desert
Tabuk

SAUDI

Qasr Farafra
Farafra Oasis
Western Desert
EGYPT
Asyut
Al Ghurdaqah
Duba
ARABIA

Libyan Desert

Sawhaj
Qina
Bur Safajah
Al Wajh
Hijaz

Mut Dakhla Oasis
Al Kharijah
Luxor
Al Qusayr
Red Sea

The Great Oasis
Idfu
Marsa al'Alam

Aswan

Tropic of Cancer
Hadabat al Jilf al Kabir

Lake Nasser
Bi'r Shalatayn

Abu Sunbul
Under Sudanese Administration

N
W E
S

Al 'Uwaynat
Lake Nuba
Wadi Halfa
Nubian Desert
Jedda

Nile Delta

Kerma
SUDAN
Port Sudan

Sahara
Red Sea

Ed Debba

This satellite image shows the river Nile as it threads across the desert. Note the way the valley fans out into a delta as the Nile reaches the sea.

Key to symbols

■	Capital city	∿ River
○	Main city/town	Jabal Katrina 2637 Mountain and height in metres
○	Other city/town	

— Country boundary
— Road
⊢⊣ Railway
∿ Canal
⊕ Airport
Lake
Seasonal lake

Land height above sea level in metres

over 5000
3000 – 5000
2000 – 3000
1000 – 2000
500 – 1000
200 – 500
0 – 200

Land below sea level

0   100   200   300   400   500 km

Scale : One centimetre on this map is the same as 75 kilometres on the ground.

A   B   C   D

SUDAN

Juba
Yei
Kapoeta

ELEMI TRIANGLE
Under Kenyan
Admin.

Lokichokio

East Africa is famous for grasslands and wild animals. Lake Victoria, high in the plains, is the source of the River Nile. It is almost as big as Scotland.

DEMOCRATIC REPUBLIC OF THE CONGO

Arua
R. Albert Nile
Kinyeti 3187

Kitgum
Gulu
Lira

Lodwar
Lake Turkana

Moyale
Kalacha Dida

Garbahaarey
Baydhabo

Hoima
Lake Albert
Fort Portal

Moroto
Soroti

R. Turkwel

Mount Nyiru 2742

Buna
El Wak

Baardheere

Bunia
Iambasa

UGANDA
Lake Kyoga

Mbale
Mount Elgon 4321

Kitale

Marsabit

Wajir

SOMALIA

Bu'aale

Margherita Peak 5110
Beni
Equator

Kampala
Kasese
Entebbe

Tororo
Jinja

Eldoret

KENYA

Maralal

R. Ewaso Ngiro

Jilib

Lake dward

Masaka

Kisumu

Nanyuki
Nakuru
Nyeri

Meru
Mount Kenya 5199
Embu

R. Tana

Garissa

Kismaayo

Lake

Ntungamo

Kisii

Narok

Thika
Machakos

Bura

Kabale
Lake Kivu

Kigali
Kibungo

Bukoba

Victoria

Nairobi

Magadi

Makindu

Garsen

Pate Island
Lamu

N

Bukavu
RWANDA
Butare
Muyinga
BURUNDI
Bujumbura

Bilharamulo

Mwanza

Nansio
Geita

Musoma

Bunda

Lake Natron

Lake Eyasi
Shinyanga

Arusha
Meru 4565

Kilimanjaro 5892

Voi
R. Galana

Malindi

W   E

S

oma

Kasulu
Kigoma

R. Gombe

Urambo
Tabora

Singida

Babati

Kondoa

Naberera

Masai Steppe
Kibaya

Korogwe

Tanga

Wete
Pemba Island

Mombasa

4° S

INDIAN OCEAN

lemie
Karema

R. Ugalla

Ikungu

Rungwa
R. Rungwa

TANZANIA

Kilosa

Zanzibar
Zanzibar Island

There are over one million Masai in Kenya and Tanzania. They keep their old customs and earn their living by herding cattle.

EMOCRATIC REPUBLIC OF THE CONGO
Lake Tanganyika
Sumbawanga

Lake Rukwa

R. Great Ruaha

Dodoma

Bagamoyo
Morogoro
Dar es Salaam

weto

Mpanda

Iringa
Mafinga

R. Rufiji

Mohoro

R. Matandu

ake weru

Mbala

Mbeya

Njombe

lke

Kapatu

Nakonde

Isoka

Karonga
MALAWI
Nyika Plateau 2527

Songea

Lindi

Luwingu
Kasama

ZAMBIA

Rumphi
Mzuzu

Lake Nyasa

Tunduru
R. Ruvuma
Negomane

Mueda

Lake angweulu
Nsombo
Chilubi

Shiwa Ngandu
Chambeshi

R. Lurio

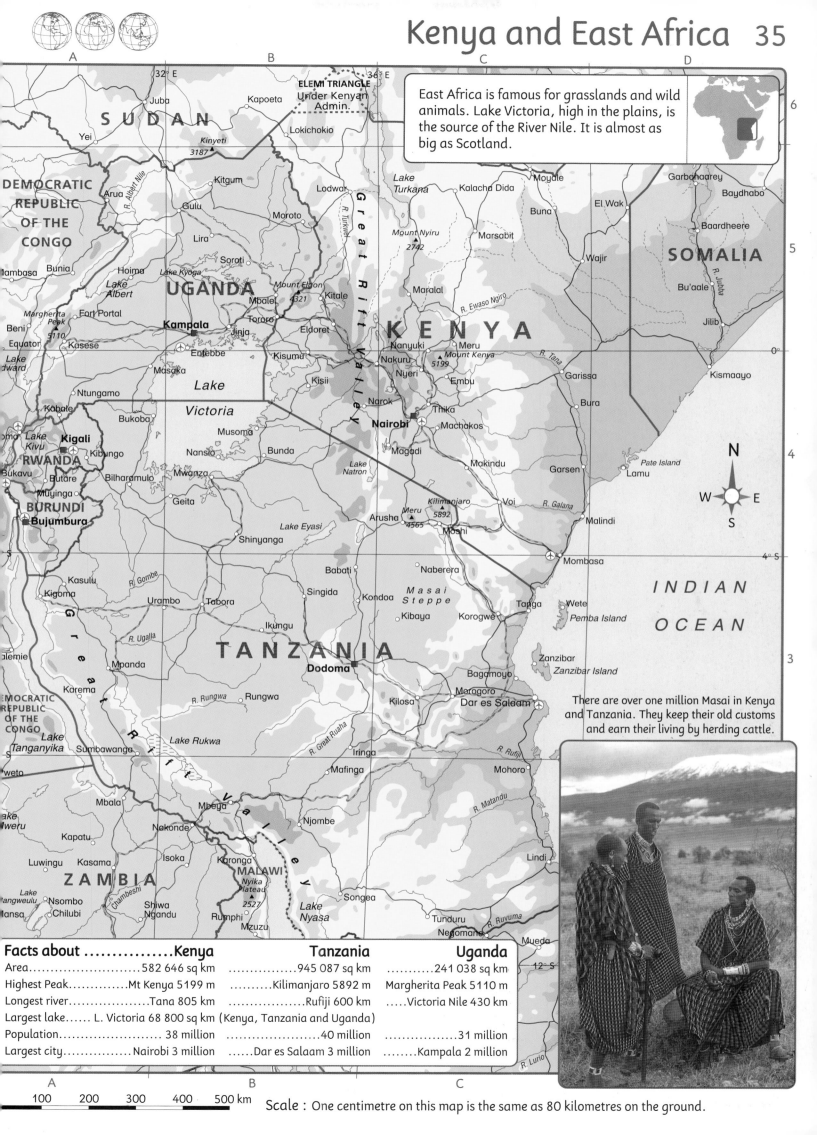

Facts about .... Kenya | Tanzania | Uganda

	Kenya	Tanzania	Uganda
Area	582 646 sq km	945 087 sq km	241 038 sq km
Highest Peak	Mt Kenya 5199 m	Kilimanjaro 5892 m	Margherita Peak 5110 m
Longest river	Tana 805 km	Rufiji 600 km	Victoria Nile 430 km
Largest lake	L. Victoria 68 800 sq km (Kenya, Tanzania and Uganda)		
Population	38 million	40 million	31 million
Largest city	Nairobi 3 million	Dar es Salaam 3 million	Kampala 2 million

A   B   C

100   200   300   400   500 km

Scale : One centimetre on this map is the same as 80 kilometres on the ground.

There are 49 countries in Asia. India, China and the Russian Federation are the largest. Singapore is the smallest. Some are islands. See how many you can find on the map.

Country with most people
China 1313 million

Largest country
Russian Federation 17 million sq km

Russian Federation
Area 17 million sq km
Population 143 million

ARCTIC OCEAN

E U R O P E

R U S S I A N   F E D E R A T I O N

Yakutsk

Sea of Okhotsk

St Petersburg

Moscow

Sakhalin

Total population of Asia
(including Russian Federation)
4172 million

Perm

Chelyabinsk

Omsk

Novosibirsk

Irkutsk

Lake Baikal

Sapporo

Volgograd

Black Sea

Ankara

TURKEY

CYPRUS

LEBANON

ISRAEL

SYRIA

JORDAN

Baghdad

IRAQ

KUWAIT

Kuwait

Riyadh

SAUDI ARABIA

BAHRAIN

QATAR

UNITED ARAB EMIRATES

Tehran

Ashgabat

TURKMENISTAN

1
2
3

Caspian Sea

KAZAKHSTAN

Astana

Aral Sea

Lake Balkhash

UZBEKISTAN

Tashkent

Almaty

Ürümqi

5

4

Ulan Bator

MONGOLIA

Harbin

Shenyang

Beijing

Tianjin

Pyongyang

NORTH KOREA

Seoul

SOUTH KOREA

Sea of Japan (East Sea)

JAPAN

Tokyo

Kobe

Osaka

Fukuoka

Kabul

AFGHANISTAN

Islamabad

Lahore

PAKISTAN

Delhi

New Delhi

Karachi

Muscat

OMAN

San'a

YEMEN

Aden

Red Sea

AFRICA

IRAN

Lanzhou

Xi'an

C H I N A

Chongqing

Nanjing

Wuhan

Shanghai

Guangzhou

Hong Kong

Largest city
Tokyo 35 million

T'aipei

TAIWAN

PACIFIC OCEAN

NEPAL

BHUTAN

BANGLADESH

Dhaka

I N D I A

Kolkata

MYANMAR (BURMA)

Nay Pyi Taw

Yangon

Hanoi

LAOS

Vientiane

VIETNAM

Luzon

PHILIPPINES

Manila

Mindanao

Davao

Mumbai

Hyderabad

Chennai

Arabian Sea

Socotra (Yemen)

Bay of Bengal

THAILAND

Bangkok

CAMBODIA

Phnom Penh

Ho Chi Minh City

South China Sea

BRUNEI

1 GEORGIA
2 ARMENIA
3 AZERBAIJAN
4 TAJIKISTAN
5 KYRGYZSTAN

Sri Jayewardenepura Kotte

SRI LANKA

Colombo

MALDIVES

Andaman Is (India)

Nicobar Is (India)

MALAYSIA

Kuala Lumpur

Putrajaya

SINGAPORE

Sumatra

Borneo

Celebes

Makassar

I N D O N E S I A

Dili

EAST TIMOR

Jakarta

Java

Surabaya

INDIAN OCEAN

Half the people in the world live in Asia, many of them in India and China.

AUSTRALIA

Key to symbols

▧ Countries

■ Capital city

○ Important city/town

0 500 1000 1500 2000 2500 3000 3500 4000 km

In the centre of Asia, the Himalayas form the largest mountain range in the world. The Gobi desert and forests of Siberia lie to the north. Southeast Asia is dotted with islands.

Total area of Asia
45 million sq km

Largest lake
Caspian Sea 371 000 sq km

Lowest point
Dead Sea
420 metres below
sea level

Longest river
Chang Jiang 6380 km

Highest mountain
Mount Everest 8848 m

Largest island
Borneo 745 561 sq km

ARCTIC OCEAN

EUROPE

Ural Mountains

Black Sea

Caspian Lowland

Caspian Sea

Aral Sea

Caucasus

Elburz Mountains

Zagros Mountains

Dead Sea

R. Euphrates

R. Tigris

The Gulf

Arabian Peninsula

Red Sea

Gulf of Aden

AFRICA

Arabian Sea

R. Indus

Thar Desert

Deccan

Sri Lanka

West Siberian Plain

R. Ob

R. Irtysh

R. Yenisey

Central Siberian Plateau

R. Lena

Siberia

R. Angara

R. Lena

R. Yenisey

Lake Baikal

R. Selenga

R. Argun

R. Amur

Altai Mts

Lake Balkhash

Ysyk-Köl

Tien Shan

Tarim Basin

Gobi Desert

Hindu Kush

K2 8611

Kunlun Shan

Plateau of Tibet

Himalaya

Annapurna 8091

Mount Everest 8848

R. Ganges

Huang He

Chang Jiang

R. Irrawaddy

Bay of Bengal

R. Mekong

Sea of Okhotsk

Sakhalin

Hokkaido

Sea of Japan (East Sea)

Honshu

Kyushu

East China Sea

Taiwan

South China Sea

PACIFIC OCEAN

Luzon

Philippines

Mindanao

Borneo

Celebes

Sumatra

Java

INDIAN OCEAN

AUSTRALIA

This satellite image shows the delta of the River Ganges in Bangladesh. This is one of the most densely populated areas in the world.

BANGLADESH

Bay of Bengal

Key to symbols

Land height above sea level in metres

over 5000
2000 – 5000
1000 – 2000
500 – 1000
200 – 500
0 – 200

Mount Everest 8848 — Mountain and height in metres

— River
Lake
Seasonal lake
Ice cap
Land below sea level

Scale : One centimetre on this map is the same as 500 kilometres on the ground.

500 1000 1500 2000 2500 3000 3500 4000 km

Africa, Asia and Europe join together in the Middle East. Many ancient civilizations grew up here. Today, the differences between people and religions have led to terrible conflicts.

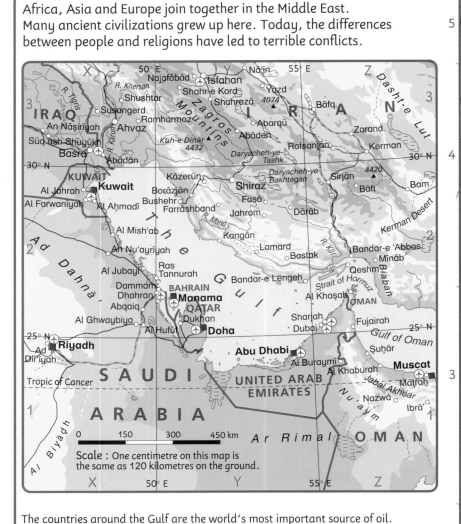

Scale : One centimetre on this map is the same as 120 kilometres on the ground.

The countries around the Gulf are the world's most important source of oil.

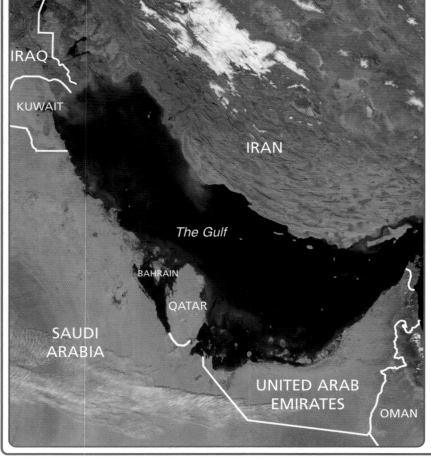

Key to symbols

■ Capital city	☐ Ice cap
○ Main city/town	*Mount Everest* ▲ 8848 Mountain and height in metres
○ Other city/town	
— Country boundary	Land height above sea level in metres
— Road	over 5000
— Railway	3000 – 5000
⋏ Canal	2000 – 3000
	1000 – 2000
⊕ Airport	500 – 1000
⬡ Lake	200 – 500
⬡ Seasonal lake	0 – 200
— River	Land below sea level

Scale : One centimetre on this map is the same as 200 kilometres on the ground.

0   200   400   600   800   1000   1200 km

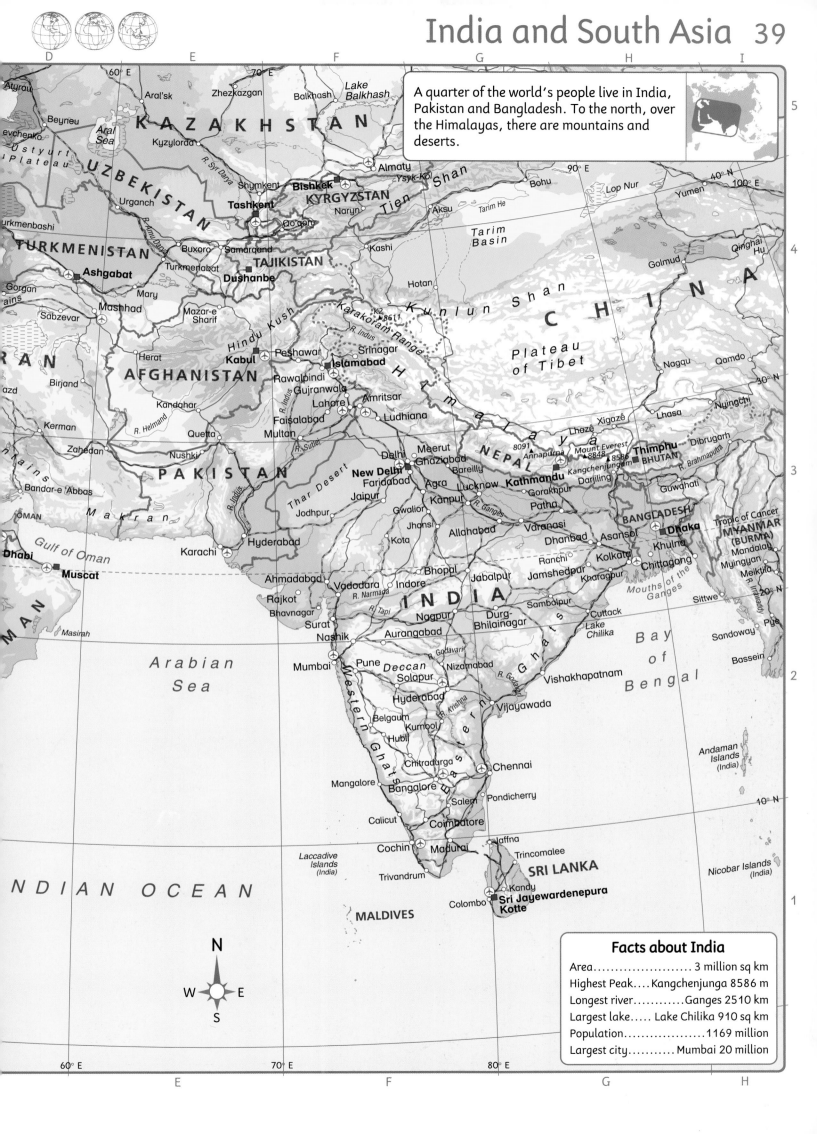

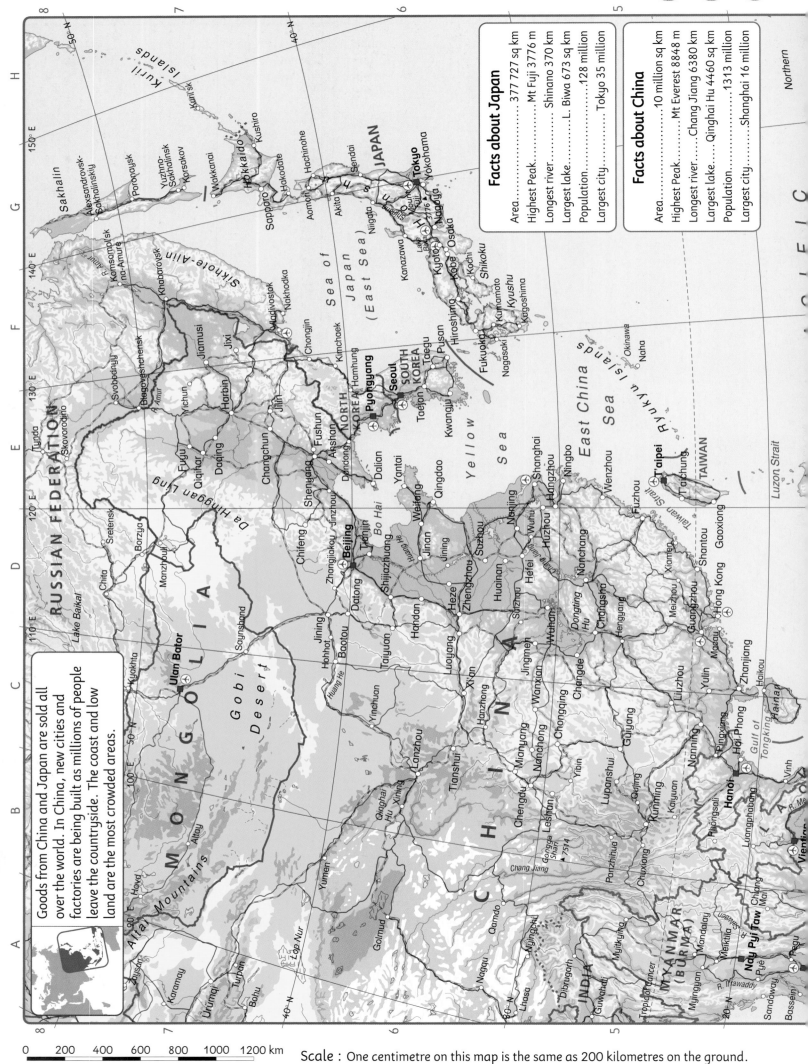

Facts about Japan

Area................377 727 sq km
Highest Peak.........Mt Fuji 3776 m
Longest river..........Shinano 370 km
Largest lake.....L. Biwa 673 sq km
Population............128 million
Largest city.......Tokyo 35 million

Facts about China

Area..............10 million sq km
Highest Peak........Mt Everest 8848 m
Longest river.....Chang Jiang 6380 km
Largest lake.....Qinghai Hu 4460 sq km
Population...........1313 million
Largest city.......Shanghai 16 million

Goods from China and Japan are sold all over the world. In China, new cities and factories are being built as millions of people leave the countryside. The coast and low land are the most crowded areas.

Scale : One centimetre on this map is the same as 200 kilometres on the ground.

0   200   400   600   800   1000 1200 km

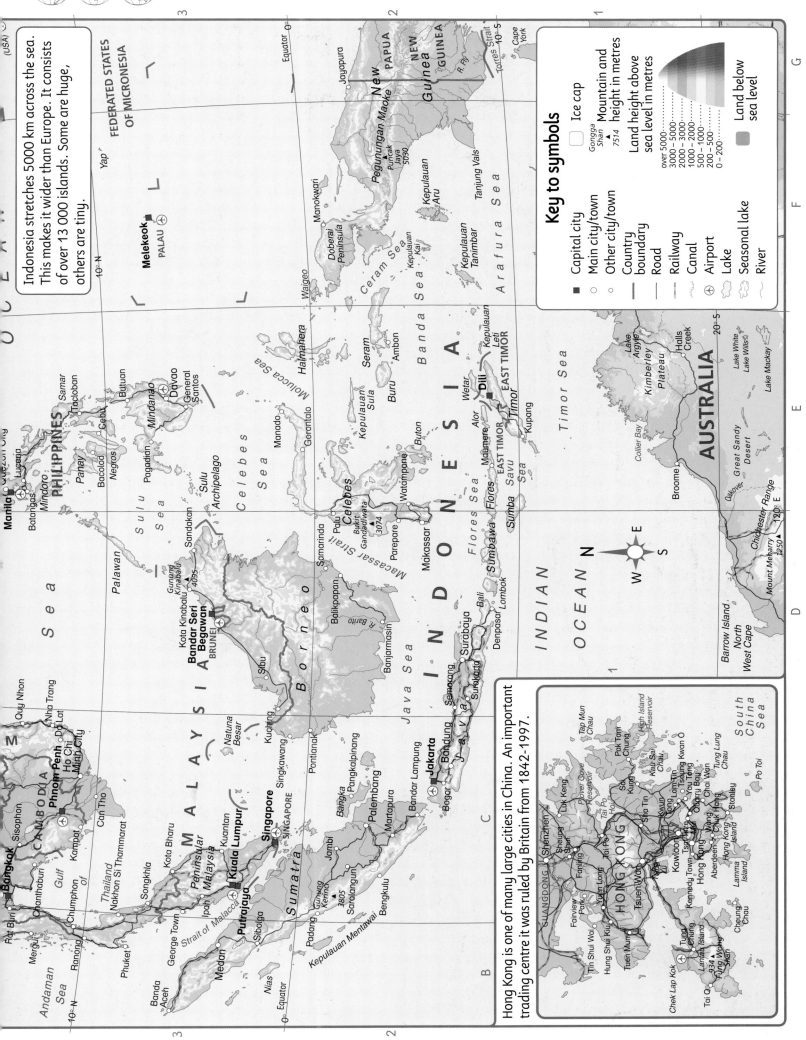

Canada, Mexico and the USA make up most of North America. Many small countries are found in the narrow belt of land which leads to South America and in the Caribbean Sea.

ARCTIC OCEAN

GREENLAND
(Denmark)

Baffin Bay

Total population of North America
528 million

ALASKA U.S.A.

Anchorage

Nuuk
(Godthåb)

Iqaluit

Great Bear Lake

Great Slave Lake

Hudson Bay

Largest country
Canada 10 million sq km

C A N A D A

St John's

Edmonton

Calgary

Vancouver

Quebec

Seattle

Winnipeg

Montreal

Halifax

Portland

Lake Superior

Lake Huron

Ottawa

Boston

Toronto

Lake Ontario

Minneapolis

Lake Michigan

New York

ATLANTIC OCEAN

PACIFIC OCEAN

Chicago

Detroit

Lake Erie

Pittsburgh

Washington D.C.

Sacramento

U N I T E D   S T A T E S

San Francisco

Salt Lake City

Denver

Kansas City

St Louis

Bermuda (UK)

O F   A M E R I C A

Los Angeles

San Diego

Phoenix

Atlanta

Country with most people
USA 306 million

El Paso

Dallas

Houston

New Orleans

Miami

THE BAHAMAS

ANTIGUA AN BARBUDA

Monterrey

Gulf of Mexico

Nassau

DOMINICAN REPUBLIC

Havana

CUBA

HAITI

PUERTO RICO (USA)

DOMINICA

ST LUCIA

BARB

Largest city
Mexico City 21 million

M E X I C O

JAMAICA

Kingston

Caribbean Sea

GRENADA

Guadalajara

Mexico City

Puebla

BELIZE

HONDURAS

GUATEMALA

Guatemala City

NICARAGUA

EL SALVADOR

Managua

Panama City

COSTA RICA

PANAMA

SOUTH

Manhattan in the centre of New York is a centre for business and entertainment.

AMERICA

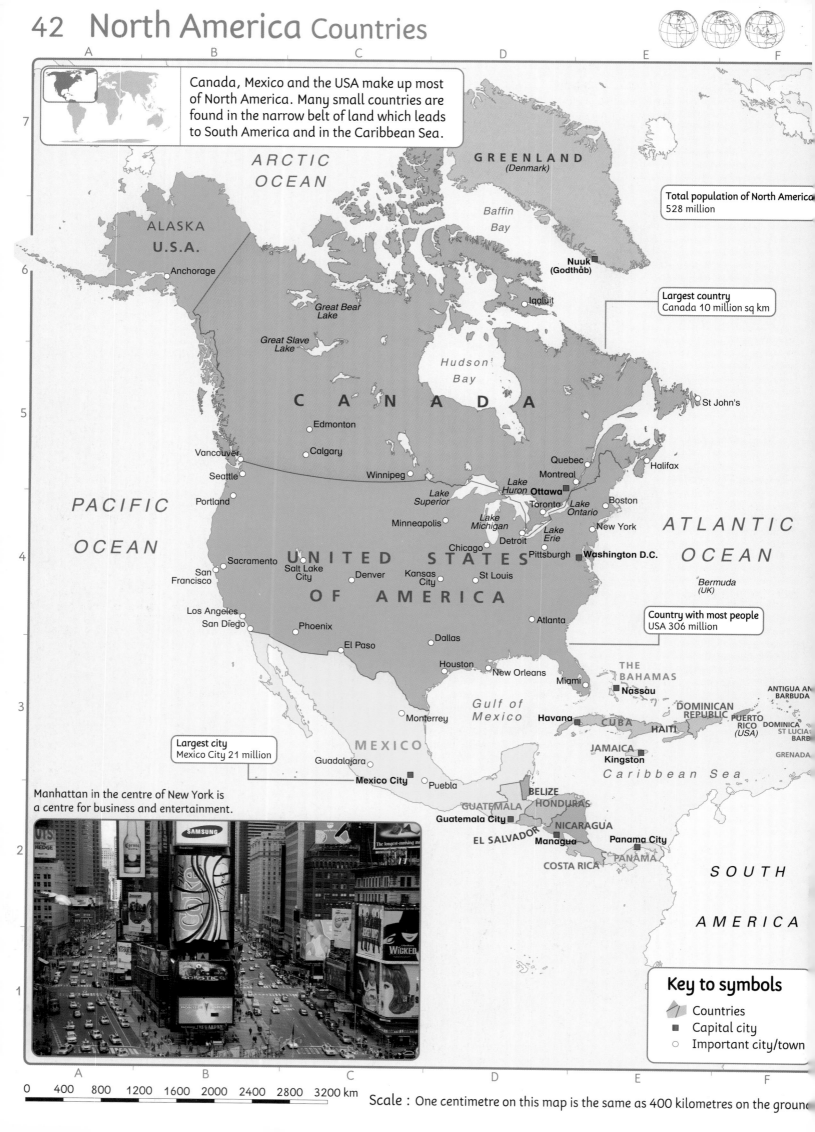

Key to symbols

◢ Countries

■ Capital city

○ Important city/town

0 400 800 1200 1600 2000 2400 2800 3200 km

Scale : One centimetre on this map is the same as 400 kilometres on the ground

The Rocky Mountains stretch down the western side of North America. Further east there are lakes and plains. In the north, Greenland is covered in ice.

ARCTIC OCEAN

Greenland

Ellesmere Island

Baffin Bay

Baffin Island

Davis Strait

Total area of North America
25 million sq km

Largest island
Greenland 2 million sq km

Cape Farewell

Victoria Island

R. Yukon

▲ Mount McKinley
6194

Gulf of Alaska

▲ Mount Logan
5959

R. Mackenzie

Great Bear Lake

Great Slave Lake

Largest lake
Lake Superior 82 100 sq km

Labrador

Newfoundland

Highest mountain
Mount McKinley 6194 m

Coast Mountains

R. Peace

Rocky Mountains

3954 ▲

Hudson Bay

Canadian Shield

PACIFIC OCEAN

Great Plains

Lake Superior

Lake Huron

R. St. Lawrence

Lake Ontario

Cape Cod

ATLANTIC OCEAN

Lowest point
Death Valley
86 metres below
sea level

R. Snake

Great Lakes

Lake Michigan

Lake Erie

Niagara Falls

Great Salt Lake

R. North Platte

R. Missouri

Mount
Elbert ▲
4398

Appalachian Mountains

Great Basin

Death Valley

Grand Canyon

R. Ohio

2037 ▲

Longest river
Mississippi-Missouri 5969 km

Mount
Whitney ▲
4418

R. Colorado

R. Red

R. Mississippi

Key to symbols

Land height above sea level in metres

over 5000
2000 – 5000
1000 – 2000
500 – 1000
200 – 500
0 – 200

Mount McKinley ▲
6194

Mountain and height in metres

River

Lake

Seasonal lake

Ice cap

Land below sea level

Gulf of California

Sierra Madre Occidental

Sierra Madre Oriental

R. Brazos

Rio Grande

Florida

Gulf of Mexico

Cuba

Hispaniola

Caribbean Sea

Yucatán

Popocatépetl ▲
5452

Lake Nicaragua

Isthmus of Panama

he Grand Canyon on the Colorado River is 1500 metres deep and
ver 400 km long. It was one of the first National Parks in the USA.

SOUTH AMERICA

400 800 1200 1600 2000 2400 2800 3200 km

Scale : One centimetre on this map is the same as 400 kilometres on the ground.

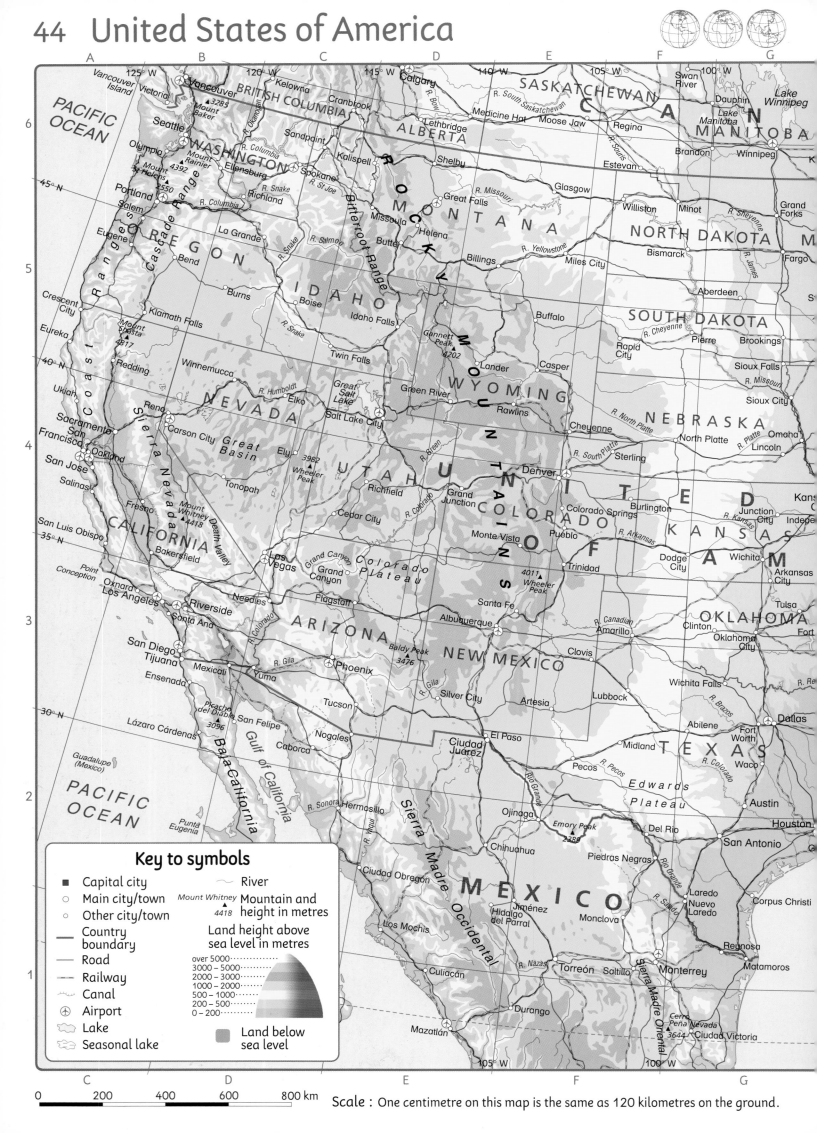

Key to symbols

- ■ Capital city
- ○ Main city/town
- ○ Other city/town
- ▬ Country boundary
- ── Road
- ── Railway
- ∿ Canal
- ⊕ Airport
- ◇ Lake
- ◇ Seasonal lake

- ⌒ River
- ▲ *Mount Whitney* Mountain and height in metres
  4418

Land height above sea level in metres

- over 5000
- 3000 – 5000
- 2000 – 3000
- 1000 – 2000
- 500 – 1000
- 200 – 500
- 0 – 200

Land below sea level

Scale : One centimetre on this map is the same as 120 kilometres on the ground.

0   200   400   600   800 km

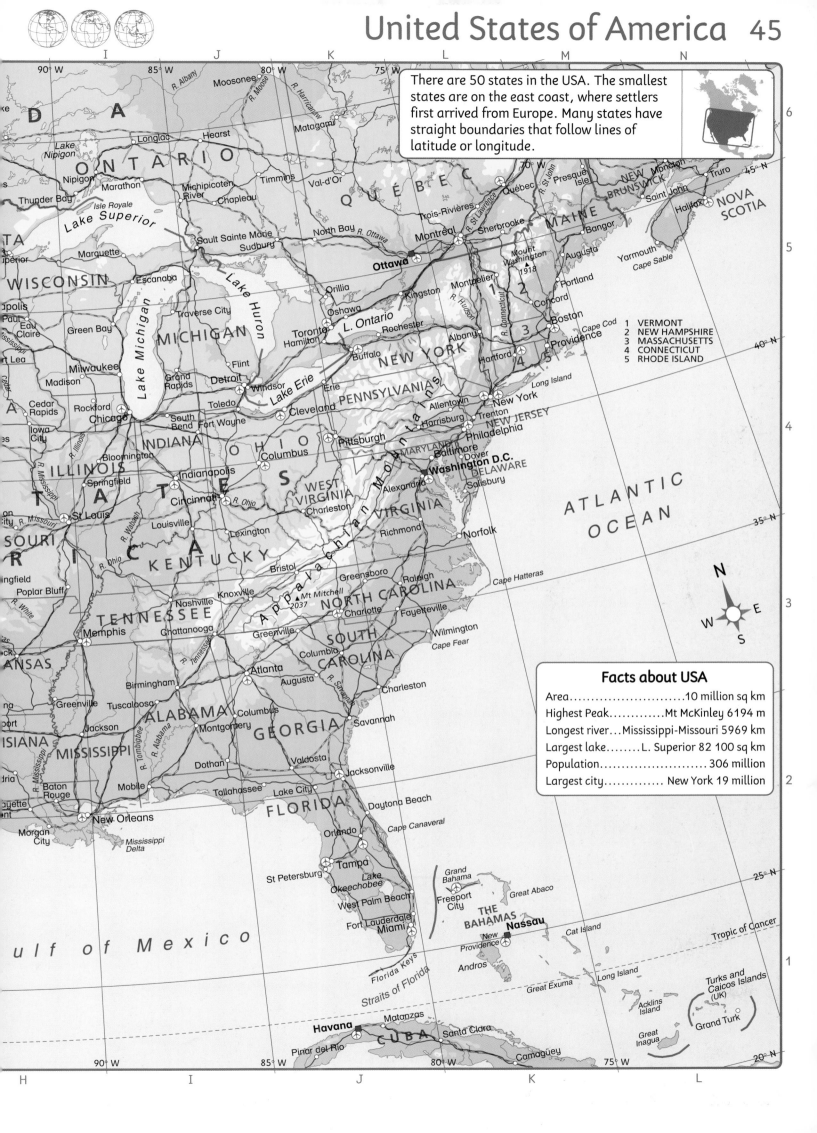

Key to symbols

- ■ Capital city
- ○ Main city/town
- ○ Other city/town
- — Country boundary
- — Road
- ⊣⊢ Railway
- ∿ Canal
- ⊕ Airport
- Lake
- Seasonal lake
- ∿ River
- Popocatépetl ▲ 5452 Mountain and height in metres

Land height above sea level in metres

- over 5000
- 3000 – 5000
- 2000 – 3000
- 1000 – 2000
- 500 – 1000
- 200 – 500
- 0 – 200

Map labels:

UNITED STATES OF AMERICA

ARIZONA · NEW MEXICO · TEXAS · ARKANSAS · MISSISSIPPI · LOUISIANA

Tijuana · Mexicali · Ensenada · Picacho del Diablo 3096 · San Felipe · Caborca · Nogales · Tucson · Silver City · El Paso · Ciudad Juárez · Artesia · Fort Worth · Dallas · Abilene · Midland · Waco · Austin · Houston · Shreveport · Jackson · Mobile · Alexandria · Baton Rouge · New Orleans

Lázaro Cárdenas · Hermosillo · R. Sonora · Guaymas · Ciudad Obregón · Santa Rosalía · Los Mochis · Chihuahua · Ojinaga · Emory Peak 2389 · Del Rio · Pecos · San Antonio · Piedras Negras · Laredo · Nuevo Laredo · Corpus Christi · Galveston · Morgan City

Punta Eugenia · Villa Insurgentes · La Paz · Culiacán · Jiménez · Hidalgo del Parral · Monclova · Reynosa · Matamoros

Cabo Falso · San José del Cabo · Mazatlán · Durango · Torreón · Saltillo · Monterrey · Cerro Peña Nevada 3644 · Ciudad Victoria · Tampico

Islas Revillagigedo (Mexico) · Tepic · Aguascalientes · San Luis Potosí · Ciudad de Valles · Poza Rica · Mérida

Puerto Vallarta · Guadalajara · Irapuato · León · Querétaro · Morelia · Toluca · Mexico City · Popocatépetl 5452 · Puebla · Orizaba · Veracruz · Coatzacoalcos · Campeche · Campeche Bay · Yucatán · Chetumal

Colima · Lázaro Cárdenas · Acapulco · Oaxaca · Juchitán · Villahermosa · Escárcega · Belmopan

Puerto Ángel · Gulf of Tehuantepec · Tuxtla Gutiérrez · GUATEMALA · Guatemala City · Santa Ana · San Salvador · EL SALVADOR · Tegucigalpa

MEXICO · Sierra Madre Occidental · Sierra Madre Oriental · Sierra Madre del Sur · R. Nazas · R. Balsas · Baja California · Gulf of California · Tropic of Cancer

Gulf of Mexico · PACIFIC OCEAN

Hurricane Katrina destroyed New Orleans in August 2005. The centre of the storm shows up clearly in this photograph from the air.

Tracks of major hurricanes

UNITED STATES OF AMERICA · ATLANTIC OCEAN · Bermuda (UK) · Gulf of Mexico · BAHAMAS · CUBA · MEXICO · BELIZE · GUATEMALA · HONDURAS · EL SALVADOR · NICARAGUA · JAMAICA · HAITI · DOMINICAN REP. · Caribbean Sea · PACIFIC OCEAN · COSTA RICA · PANAMA · VENEZUELA

- → Gordon 199
- → Fran 1996
- → Mitch 1998
- → Floyd 1999
- → Isabel 2003
- → Charley 200
- → Katrina 200
- → Rita 2005
- → Dean 2007

0 200 400 600 800 km

Scale : One centimetre on this map is the same as 135 kilometres on the ground.

Mexico is eight times the size of the UK. With many high mountains, it has a population of over 100 million people. The Caribbean Sea to the east is dotted with islands. These are popular with tourists.

N W E S

ATLANTIC OCEAN

85° W 80° W 75° W 70° W 65° W 60° W

25° N
Tropic of Cancer
20° N
15° N
10° N

Atlanta
Augusta
Columbus
ntgomery
SOUTH CAROLINA
Charleston
Savannah
GEORGIA
Valdosta
hassee
Lake City
Jacksonville
FLORIDA
Daytona Beach
Orlando
Cape Canaveral
St Petersburg
Tampa
Lake Okeechobee
West Palm Beach
Fort Lauderdale
Miami
Florida Keys
Straits of Florida

Grand Bahama
Freeport City
Great Abaco
THE BAHAMAS
New Providence
Nassau
Cat Island
Andros
Great Exuma
Long Island
Acklins Island
Turks and Caicos Islands (UK)
Grand Turk

Havana
Matanzas
Pinar del Río
Guane
Santa Clara
CUBA
Cabo
ntonio
Isla de la Juventud
Camagüey
Holguín
Bayamo
Guantánamo
Sa Maestra
Santiago de Cuba
Port-de-Paix
Cap-Haïtien
Santiago
Jérémie
HAITI
Pico Duarte 3175
Port-au-Prince
Santo Domingo
DOMINICAN REPUBLIC
Hispaniola
Ponce
San Juan
PUERTO RICO (USA)
Virgin Is (UK)
Virgin Is (USA)

Cayman Islands (UK)
Montego Bay
JAMAICA
Kingston
Greater

Great Inagua

Leeward Islands
Anguilla (UK)
St-Martin (Fr.)
Sint Maarten (Neth.)
Barbuda
ANTIGUA AND BARBUDA
St John's
Antigua
ST KITTS AND NEVIS
Montserrat (UK)
Guadeloupe (Fr.)
DOMINICA
Roseau
Martinique (Fr.)
Castries
ST LUCIA
Kingstown
ST VINCENT AND THE GRENADINES
GRENADA
St George's
Windward Is
BARBADOS
Bridgetown

Antilles

Caribbean

Lesser Antilles

Sea

Lesser Antilles

Punta Gallinas
Aruba (Neth.)
Netherlands Antilles
Curaçao
TRINIDAD Tobago & TOBAGO
Port of Spain
Güiria Trinidad

CARAGUA
Rio Grande
nagua
Lake
agua
COSTA RICA
San José
Chirripo 3819
Panama Canal
Colón
Isthmus of Panama
David
Aguadulce
PANAMA
Panama City
Turbo

Ríohacha
Barranquilla
Cartagena
Valledupar
Sincelejo
Montería
R. Magdalena
Coro
Maracaibo
Barquisimeto
Valencia
Maracay
Caracas
Lake Maracaibo
Acarigua
Barinas
San Cristóbal
San Fernando de Apure
COLOMBIA
Cúcuta
Bucaramanga
VENEZUELA
Cumaná
Barcelona
Maturín
R. Tigre
El Tigre
El Callao
Ciudad Bolívar
R. Orinoco
Embalse de Guri
Ciudad Guayana
Orinoco Delta

JAMAICA
Lucea
Montego Bay
Falmouth
St Ann's Bay
Oracabessa
Port Maria
Grange Hill
Negril
Cambridge
The Cockpit Country
Highgate
Annotto Bay
Port Antonio
South West Point
Savanna-la-Mar
Christiana
Ewarton
Blue Mt Peak 2256
Don Figueiro Mts
Lacovia
Chapelton
Bog Walk
Blue Mountains
Black River
Mandeville
May Pen
Spanish Town
Kingston
Bull Savannah
Portland Bight
Morant Bay
Port Morant
Portland Point

Trinidad
VENEZUELA
Diego Martin
El Tucuche 936
Mt Aripo 940
Galera Point
Port of Spain
Tunapuna
Arima
Sangre Grande
Chaguanas
Gulf of Paria
Couva
Prince's Town
Rio Claro
San Fernando
Penal
Point Fortin
Siparia
Trinity Hills 304
Galeota Point

ST LUCIA
Pointe du Cap
Cap Marquis
Castries
Anse-la-Raye
Dennery
Mount Gimie 950
Soufrière
Micoud
Choiseul
Laborie
Vieux Fort

H I J K L M

Brazil covers nearly half of South America. Argentina and Peru area also large countries. Chile is 4000 km long but only a few hundred kilometres wide.

NORTH AMERICA

Barranquilla
Maracaibo
Caracas
Port of Spain
TRINIDAD AND TOBAGO

VENEZUELA

Georgetown
GUYANA
Paramaribo
Cayenne
SURINAME
FRENCH GUIANA

Medellín
Bogotá
COLOMBIA
Cali

Quito
ECUADOR
Guayaquil

Belém
São Luís

Galapagos Islands (Ecuador)

Iquitos
Manaus

Fortaleza
Natal

B R A Z I L

Trujillo
PERU

Recife
Aracaju
Salvador

Lima

Largest country
Brazil 9 million sq km

Lake Titicaca

Brasília

Largest city
São Paulo 20 million

Country with most people
Brazil 192 million

Arequipa
BOLIVIA
La Paz

Belo Horizonte

Sucre

PARAGUAY

Antofagasta
Asunción

São Paulo
Rio de Janeiro

Curitiba

A T L A N T I C   O C E A N

Juan Fernandez Islands (Chile)

Valparaíso
Santiago

C H I L E

A R G E N T I N A

URUGUAY

Buenos Aires
Montevideo

Porto Alegre

Concepción

Mar del Plata

P A C I F I C

O C E A N

Rio de Janeiro is a huge city built around one of the best natural harbours in South America

Falkland Islands (UK)

Punta Arenas
Tierra del Fuego

Total population of South America
385 million

Key to symbols

- Countries
- ■ Capital city
- ○ Important city/town

Scale : One centimetre on this map is the same as 400 kilometres on the ground

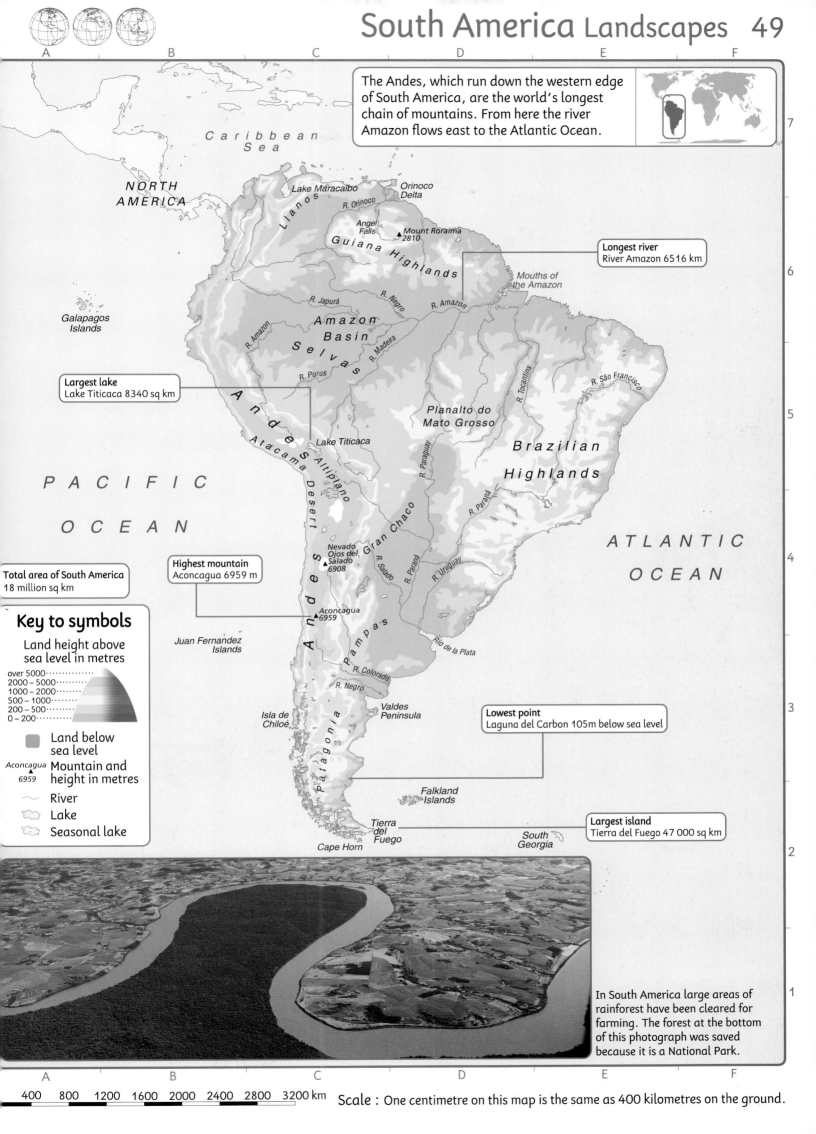

The Andes, which run down the western edge of South America, are the world's longest chain of mountains. From here the river Amazon flows east to the Atlantic Ocean.

Caribbean Sea

NORTH AMERICA

Lake Maracaibo

Orinoco Delta

R. Orinoco

Angel Falls

Mount Roraima 2810

Llanos

Guiana Highlands

Longest river
River Amazon 6516 km

Mouths of the Amazon

R. Japurá

R. Negro

R. Amazon

R. Amazon

Amazon Basin Selvas

Galapagos Islands

R. Madeira

R. Purus

R. São Francisco

Largest lake
Lake Titicaca 8340 sq km

R. Tocantins

Planalto do Mato Grosso

R. Paraguay

Brazilian Highlands

Lake Titicaca

A n d e s

Atacama Desert

Altiplano

PACIFIC OCEAN

R. Paraná

R. Paraná

R. Salado

Gran Chaco

R. Uruguay

ATLANTIC OCEAN

Total area of South America
18 million sq km

Highest mountain
Aconcagua 6959 m

Nevado Ojos del Salado 6908

Aconcagua 6959

Pampas

Rio de la Plata

Key to symbols

Land height above sea level in metres

over 5000
2000 – 5000
1000 – 2000
500 – 1000
200 – 500
0 – 200

Juan Fernandez Islands

R. Colorado

R. Negro

Lowest point
Laguna del Carbon 105m below sea level

Valdes Peninsula

Land below sea level

Aconcagua 6959 Mountain and height in metres

Isla de Chiloé

Patagonia

River

Lake

Seasonal lake

Falkland Islands

Tierra del Fuego

Cape Horn

South Georgia

Largest island
Tierra del Fuego 47 000 sq km

In South America large areas of rainforest have been cleared for farming. The forest at the bottom of this photograph was saved because it is a National Park.

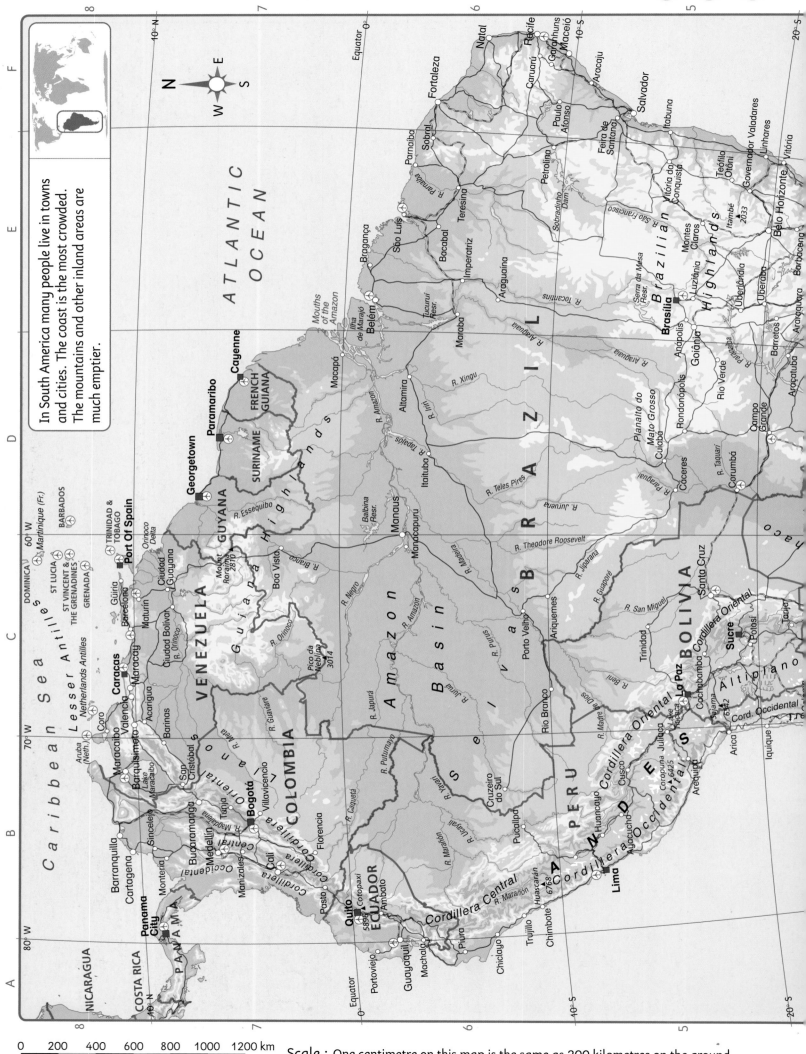

In South America many people live in towns and cities. The coast is the most crowded. The mountains and other inland areas are much emptier.

ATLANTIC OCEAN

Caribbean Sea

Lesser Antilles

Netherlands Antilles

DOMINICA
Martinique (Fr.)
ST LUCIA
ST VINCENT &
THE GRENADINES
GRENADA
BARBADOS
TRINIDAD & TOBAGO
Port Of Spain

Cayenne
FRENCH GUIANA

Paramaribo
SURINAME

Georgetown
GUYANA

Mouths of the Amazon

Ilha de Marajó

Belém

Macapá

VENEZUELA

Caracas
Valencia
Maracay
Barcelona
Maturín
Barinas
Acarigua
Coro
Maracaibo
Lake Maracaibo
Barquisimeto
Ciudad Bolívar
Ciudad Guayana
Güiria
R. Orinoco
Orinoco Delta
R. Branco
Boa Vista
R. Negro

Mount Roraima 2810

Guiana Highlands

Pico da Neblina 3014

R. Essequibo

R. Orinoco

COLOMBIA

Barranquilla
Cartagena
Sincelejo
Montería
Bucaramanga
Medellín
Manizales
Cali
Pasto
Bogotá
Tunja
Villavicencio
Florencia
San Cristóbal
R. Magdalena
R. Meta
R. Guaviare
Cordillera Occidental
Cordillera Central
Cordillera Oriental
Llanos Orientales

ECUADOR

Quito
Cotopaxi 5897
Ambato
Portoviejo
Guayaquil
Machala

Equator

R. Putumayo
R. Caquetá
R. Japurá
R. Amazon
R. Negro

AMAZON BASIN

Manaus
Manacapuru
Balbina Resr.
R. Madeira
R. Purus
R. Juruá
R. Javari
R. Ucayali
R. Marañón

PERU

Piura
Chiclayo
Trujillo
Chimbote
Huascarán 6768
Lima
Chincha
Ayacucho
Huancayo
Cusco
Arequipa
Coropuna 6425
Arica
Iquique

Cordillera Occidental
Cordillera Central
Cordillera Oriental

A N D E S

S e l v a s

Cruzeiro do Sul
Pucallpa
Rio Branco
Porto Velho
Ariquemes
R. Jiparaná
R. Theodore Roosevelt
R. Guaporé
R. Mamoré
R. Beni
R. Madre de Dios
Lake Titicaca
La Paz
Cochabamba
Sucre
Potosí
Santa Cruz
Trinidad
R. San Miguel
R. San Juan
Sajama 6542
Altiplano
Cord. Occidental
Cordillera Oriental

BOLIVIA

Tarija

B R A Z I L

Manaus
R. Amazon
R. Tapajós
R. Xingu
Altamira
Itaituba
R. Iriri
Marabá
Araguaína
R. Tocantins
R. Araguaia
Tucuruí Resr.
Imperatriz
Bacabal
Teresina
São Luís
Bragança
Parnaíba
Sobral
Fortaleza
Natal
Recife
Caruaru
Garanhuns
Maceió
Aracaju
Salvador
Itabuna
Feira de Santana
Petrolina
Paulo Afonso
Sobradinho Dam
R. São Francisco
Vitória da Conquista
Montes Claros
Luziânia
Teófilo Otoni
Governador Valadares
Linhares
Vitória
Itaúnas
Itambé 2033
Belo Horizonte
Barbacena
Brasília
Anápolis
Goiânia
Rio Verde
Rondonópolis
Cuiabá
Planalto do Mato Grosso
Serra da Mesa Resr.
R. Tocantins
Brazilian Highlands
Uberlândia
Uberaba
Araguari
Araçatuba
Campo Grande
Corumbá
Cáceres
R. Taquari
R. Paraguai
Cochabamba
Barretos
Araraquara

Chaco

PANAMA
Panama City
COSTA RICA
NICARAGUA

Scale : One centimetre on this map is the same as 200 kilometres on the ground.

0   200   400   600   800   1000   1200 km

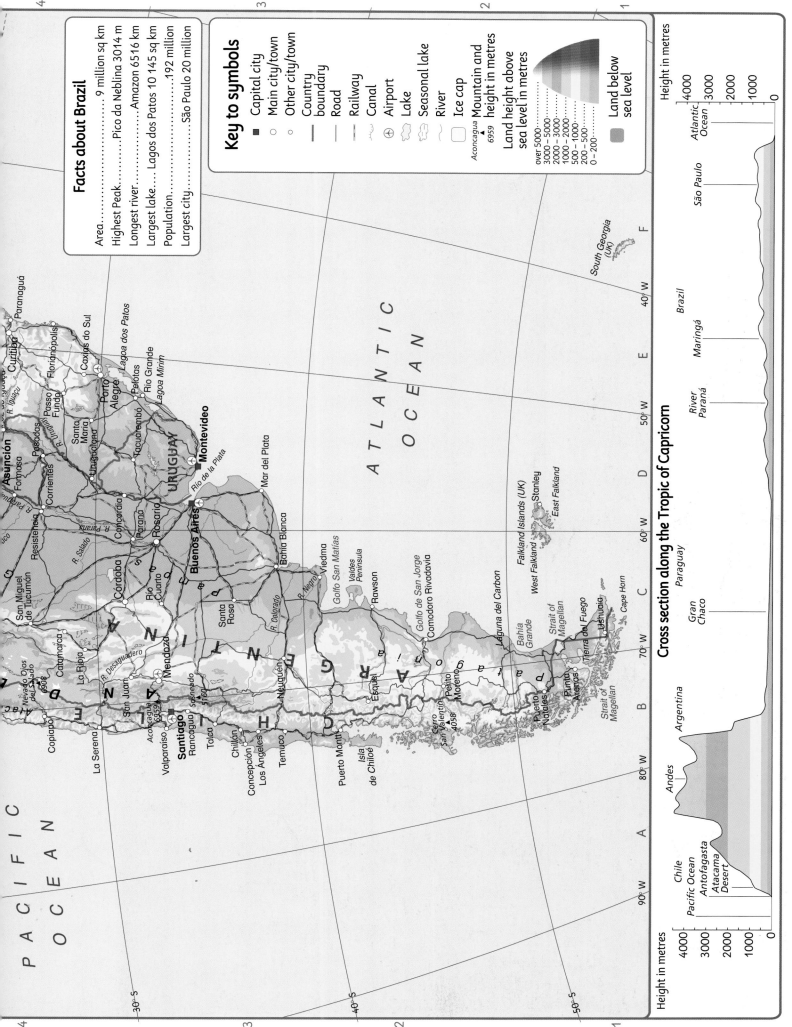

Australia, New Zealand and Papua New Guinea are the largest countries in Oceania. Other countries are made up of groups of islands scattered across the Pacific Ocean.

Key to symbols

- Countries
- ■ Capital city
- ○ Important city/town

ASIA

New Guinea

Lae

PAPUA NEW GUINEA

■ **Port Moresby**

Arafura Sea

Timor Sea

INDIAN OCEAN

○ Darwin

○ Cairns

○ Townsville

Coral Sea

○ Rockhampton

Alice Springs ○

A U S T R A L I A

Lake Eyre

○ Kalgoorlie

Great Australian Bight

○ Perth

○ Adelaide

○ Brisbane
Gold Coast

○ Newcastle
○ Sydney

■ **Canberra**

○ Melbourne

Geelong ○

Tasmania

○ Hobart

■ **Yaren**
NAURU ·

KIRIBAT

SOLOMON ISLANDS

Honiara ■

TUVA

VANUATU

■ **Port Vila**

New Caledonia (Fr.)

■ **Nouméa**

FIJI ■

P A C I F I C O C E A N

Largest country
Australia 8 million sq km

Country with most people
Australia 21 million

Tasman Sea

North Island ○ Auckland

NEW ZEALAND

■ **Wellington**

○ Christchurch

South Island

○ Dunedin

Total population of Oceania
34 million

Largest city
Sydney 5 million

Tuvalu is made up of a chain of nine small islands and coral reefs. There are only 12 000 people in the whole country.

Scale : One centimetre on this map is the same as 325 kilometres on the ground.

0 300 600 900 1200 1500 1800 2100 km

Key to symbols

Land height above sea level in metres

over 5000
2000 – 5000
1000 – 2000
500 – 1000
200 – 500
0 – 200

Puncak Jaya
▲
5030
Mountain and height in metres

River

Lake

Seasonal lake

Land below sea level

Oceania has many landscapes. Australia has many deserts, New Zealand and Papua New Guinea have high mountains and there are groups of coral islands in the Pacific Ocean.

Highest mountain
Puncak Jaya 5030 m

New Ireland

Total area of Oceania
9 million sq km

Puncak Jaya 5030 ▲
Mount Wilhelm ▲ 4509
New Guinea
New Britain
Solomon Islands

Arafura Sea

Timor Sea

Cape York Peninsula
Gulf of Carpentaria
Great Barrier Reef
Coral Sea

Largest island
New Guinea 808 510 sq km

INDIAN
OCEAN

Arnhem Land

Kimberley Plateau
R. Fitzroy

Great Sandy Desert
R. Fortescue

A u s t r a l i a
Macdonnell Ranges
867 ▲ Uluru (Ayers Rock)
Musgrave Ranges

Fiji

New Caledonia

Largest lake
Lake Eyre 8900 sq km
In dry weather Lake Eyre can dry up completely

Great Victoria Desert
Lake Eyre
Lake Torrens

Nullarbor Plain
Great Australian Bight

R. Darling
R. Macquarie
R. Lachlan
R. Murrumbidgee
R. Murray
R. Murray

Lowest point
Lake Eyre
16 metres below sea level

PACIFIC OCEAN

Cape Leeuwin

Mount Kosciuszko ▲ 2229

Longest river
Murray-Darling 3750 km

Tasman Sea

North Cape

North Island

Aoraki (Mount Cook) is the highest mountain in New Zealand. The name means 'cloud piercer' in the local language.

Tasmania

New Zealand
Aoraki (Mount Cook) ▲ 3754
South Island

Uluru (Ayers Rock) in the middle of Australia is a World Heritage site and a holy place for Aborigines.

300 600 900 1200 1500 1800 2100 km

Scale : One centimetre on this map is the same as 325 kilometres on the ground.

The Arctic Ocean is the smallest of the world's oceans. It is very cold and mostly covered with sea ice. In summer whales, seals and other creatures come to the Arctic Ocean looking for food.

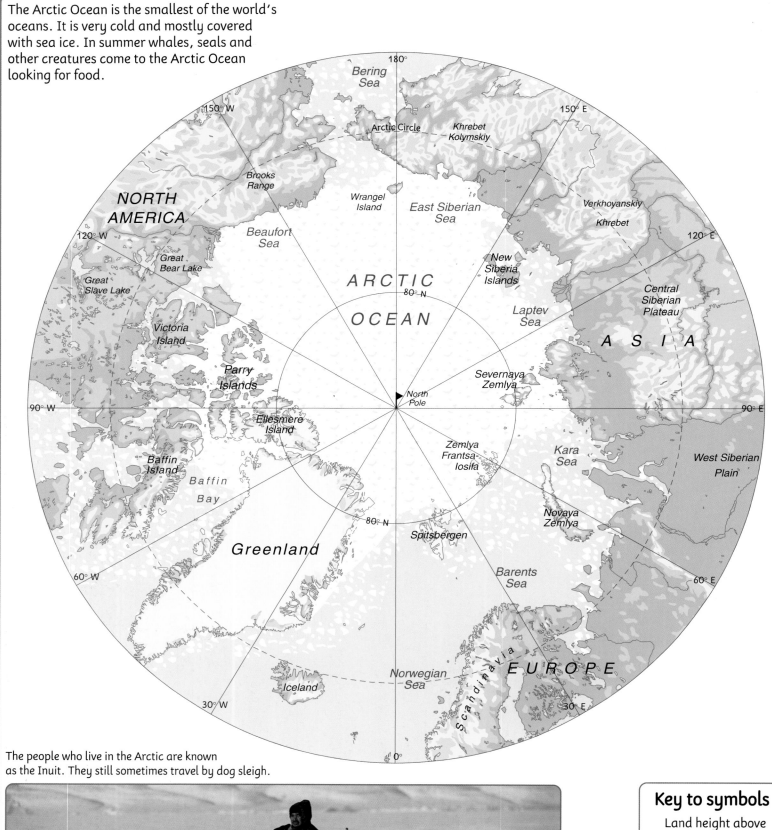

Bering Sea

180°

150° W

Arctic Circle

Khrebet Kolymskiy

150° E

Brooks Range

NORTH AMERICA

120° W

Wrangel Island

East Siberian Sea

Verkhoyanskiy Khrebet

Beaufort Sea

Great Bear Lake

New Siberia Islands

120° E

Great Slave Lake

ARCTIC

80° N

Laptev Sea

Central Siberian Plateau

Victoria Island

OCEAN

A S I A

Parry Islands

Severnaya Zemlya

90° W

North Pole

90° E

Ellesmere Island

Zemlya Frantsa-Iosifa

Kara Sea

West Siberian Plain

Baffin Island

Baffin Bay

80° N

Novaya Zemlya

Greenland

Spitsbergen

60° W

Barents Sea

60° E

Norwegian Sea

E U R O P E

30° W

Iceland

Scandinavia

30° E

0°

The people who live in the Arctic are known as the Inuit. They still sometimes travel by dog sleigh.

Key to symbols

Land height above sea level in metres

over 2000
1000 – 2000
500 – 1000
200 – 500
0 – 200

~ River
Lake
Ice cap
Polar pack ice
Drifting ice

0   500   1000   1500   2000 km

Scale : One centimetre on this map is the same as 350 kilometres on the ground.

ames of bases numbered on map
1 Presidente Eduardo Frei Montalva (Chile)
2 Comandante Ferraz (Brazil)
3 Capitan Arturo Prat (Chile)
4 Bellingshausen (Russian Federation)
5 Teniente Jubany (Argentina)
6 Arctowski (Poland)
7 General Bernardo O'Higgins (Chile)
8 Chang Cheng (Great Wall) (China)
9 Artigas (Uruguay)
10 General San Martin (Argentina)

Antarctica is the world's coldest, driest and windiest continent. It is covered by a thick sheet of ice. In many places the ice is thicker than the highest mountains in the UK. Very few plants and animals survive here.

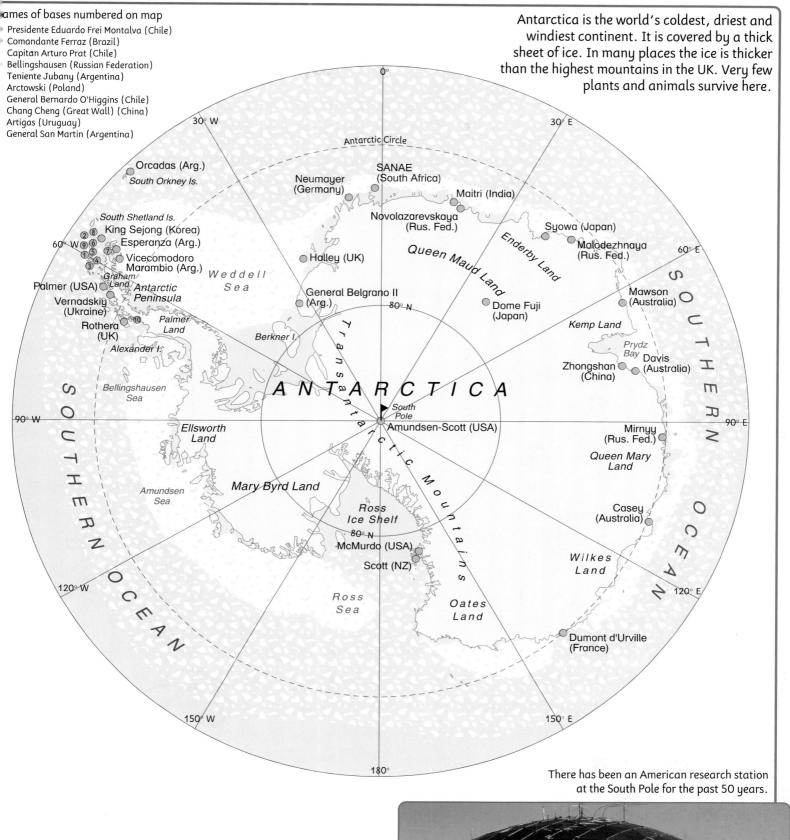

There has been an American research station at the South Pole for the past 50 years.

Key to symbols

- Ice shelf
- Ice cap
- Polar pack ice
- Drifting ice
- Manned bases

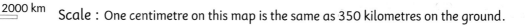

500   1000   1500   2000 km

Scale : One centimetre on this map is the same as 350 kilometres on the ground.

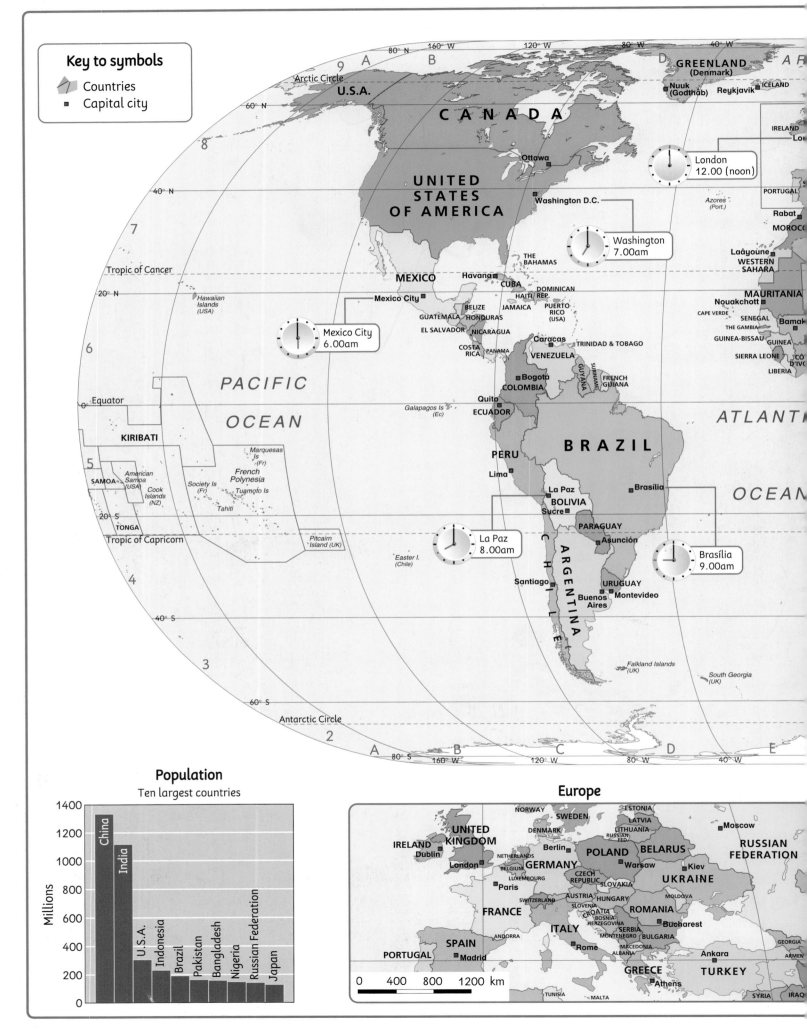

Key to symbols

◆ Countries
▪ Capital city

London 12.00 (noon)

Washington 7.00am

Mexico City 6.00am

La Paz 8.00am

Brasília 9.00am

Arctic Circle

80° N

60° N

40° N

Tropic of Cancer

20° N

Equator

20° S

Tropic of Capricorn

40° S

60° S

Antarctic Circle

80° S

U.S.A.

CANADA

GREENLAND (Denmark)

Nuuk (Godthåb)   Reykjavik   ICELAND

IRELAND   Lo

UNITED STATES OF AMERICA

Ottawa

Washington D.C.

PORTUGAL

Azores (Port.)

Rabat
MOROCC

MEXICO

Havana   CUBA

THE BAHAMAS

Mexico City

Laâyoune
WESTERN SAHARA

Hawaiian Islands (USA)

BELIZE   DOMINICAN REP.
GUATEMALA   HONDURAS   JAMAICA   HAITI   PUERTO RICO (USA)
EL SALVADOR   NICARAGUA
COSTA RICA   PANAMA

Caracas   TRINIDAD & TOBAGO
VENEZUELA   GUYANA   SURINAME   FRENCH GUIANA
Bogotá
COLOMBIA

MAURITANIA

Nouakchott
CAPE VERDE   SENEGAL   Bamak
THE GAMBIA
GUINEA-BISSAU   GUINEA   CÔ
SIERRA LEONE   D'IVO
LIBERIA

PACIFIC

OCEAN

KIRIBATI

Marquesas Is (Fr)

French Polynesia

Society Is (Fr)   Tuamoto Is
Tahiti

SAMOA   American Samoa (USA)   Cook Islands (NZ)

TONGA

Pitcairn Island (UK)

Easter I. (Chile)

Galapagos Is (Ec)

Quito
ECUADOR

PERU

Lima

La Paz
BOLIVIA
Sucre

BRAZIL

Brasília

ATLANTI

OCEAN

PARAGUAY

Asunción

CHILE

Santiago   ARGENTINA

URUGUAY
Buenos Aires   Montevideo

Falkland Islands (UK)

South Georgia (UK)

9 A   **B**   D
8
7
6
5
4
3
2
A   B   C   D   E

80° W   160° W   120° W   80° W   40° W

Population
Ten largest countries

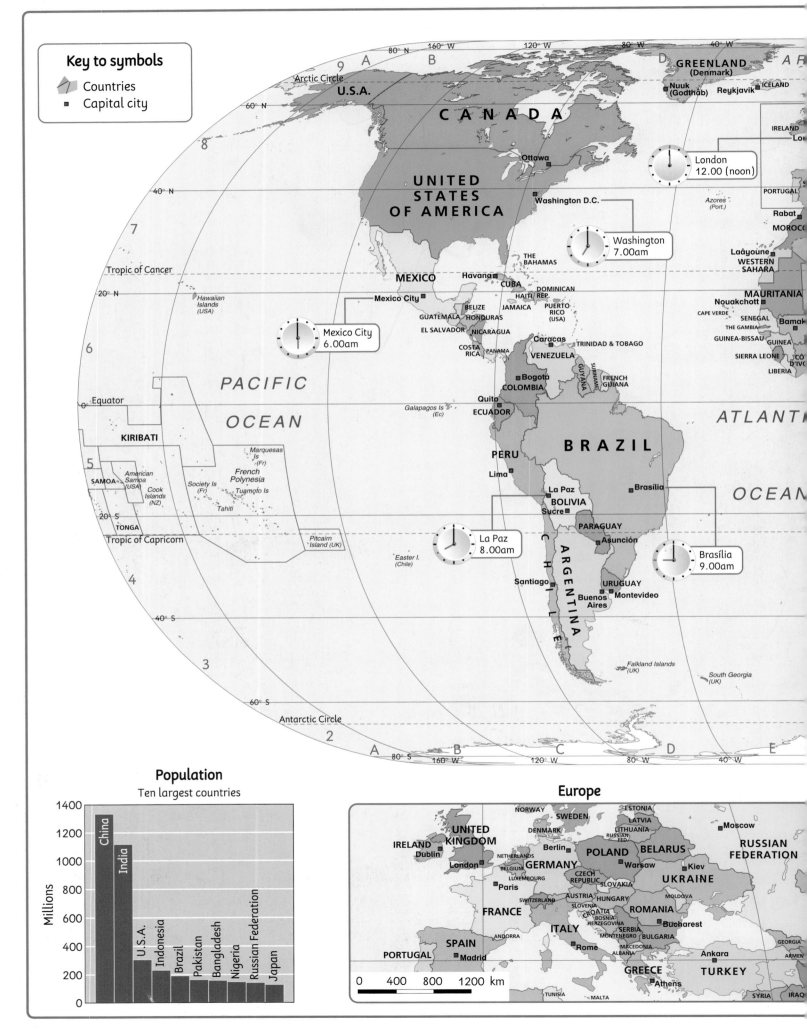

Millions

1400
1200
1000
800
600
400
200
0

China
India
U.S.A.
Indonesia
Brazil
Pakistan
Bangladesh
Nigeria
Russian Federation
Japan

Europe

NORWAY   SWEDEN   ESTONIA
LATVIA
LITHUANIA
DENMARK   RUSSIAN FED.
UNITED KINGDOM
IRELAND
Dublin   Berlin   POLAND   BELARUS   Moscow
London   NETHERLANDS   GERMANY   Warsaw   Kiev   RUSSIAN FEDERATION
BELGIUM   CZECH REPUBLIC   UKRAINE
LUXEMBOURG   SLOVAKIA
Paris   AUSTRIA   HUNGARY   MOLDOVA
SWITZERLAND   SLOVENIA   ROMANIA
FRANCE   CROATIA   GEORGIA
BOSNIA HERZEGOVINA   SERBIA   Bucharest
ITALY   MONTENEGRO   BULGARIA   ARMEN
SPAIN   ANDORRA   Rome   MACEDONIA
PORTUGAL   Madrid   ALBANIA   Ankara
GREECE   TURKEY
Athens
TUNISIA   MALTA   SYRIA   IRAQ

0   400   800   1200 km

Scale : One centimetre on this map is the same as 850 kilometres on the ground.

0   850   1700   2550   3400 km

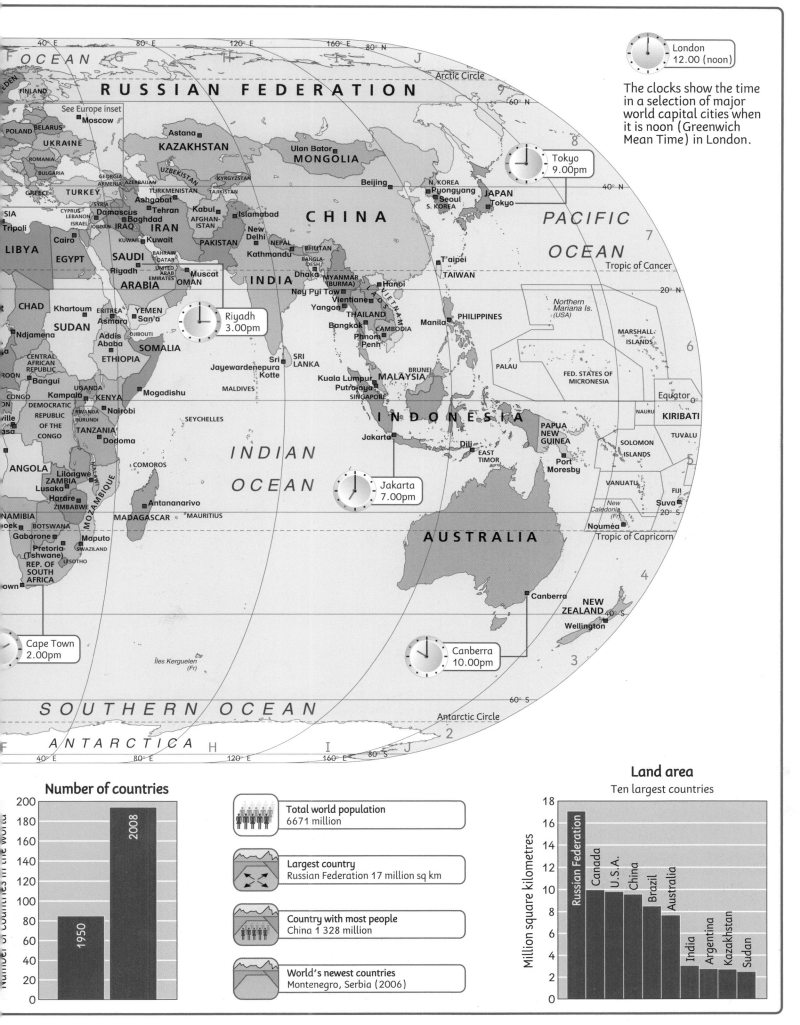

OCEAN G

40° E   80° E   120° E   160° E   80° N   J

Arctic Circle

RUSSIAN FEDERATION

EDEN
FINLAND
See Europe inset
■ Moscow
POLAND BELARUS
UKRAINE
ROMANIA
BULGARIA
GEORGIA
GREECE   TURKEY
ARMENIA AZERBAIJAN
SIA   CYPRUS SYRIA
LEBANON ■ Damascus
ISRAEL ■ Baghdad
Tripoli   JORDAN IRAQ
Cairo   KUWAIT ■ Kuwait
LIBYA   EGYPT   SAUDI
■ Riyadh
ARABIA   UNITED
ARAB   ■ Muscat
EMIRATES OMAN
CHAD   Khartoum   ERITREA   YEMEN
Ndjamena   SUDAN   Asmara   San'a DJIBOUTI
Addis
Ababa   SOMALIA
CENTRAL
AFRICAN
REPUBLIC   ETHIOPIA
ROON   ■ Bangui
CONGO   UGANDA
Kampala   KENYA
DEMOCRATIC   RWANDA   Nairobi
ville   REPUBLIC   BURUNDI
asa   OF THE   TANZANIA
CONGO   Dodoma
ANGOLA
Lilongwe
ZAMBIA
Lusaka
Harare
ZIMBABWE
NAMIBIA   BOTSWANA
ek
Gaborone   Maputo
Pretoria   SWAZILAND
(Tshwane)   LESOTHO
REP. OF
SOUTH
AFRICA
wn

Astana
KAZAKHSTAN
UZBEKISTAN
KYRGYZSTAN
ASHGABAT
TURKMENISTAN
TAJIKISTAN
Tehran   Kabul
IRAN   AFGHAN-
ISTAN   Islamabad
New
Delhi
PAKISTAN   NEPAL
Kathmandu
BAHRAIN
QATAR   Dhaka
INDIA   BANGLA-
DESH
Sri   SRI LANKA
Jayewardenepura
Kotte
MALDIVES
SEYCHELLES

Ulan Bator
MONGOLIA
Beijing ■

CHINA

BHUTAN
Nay Pyi Taw
MYANMAR
(BURMA)
Yangon
THAILAND
Bangkok ■
Phnom
Penh
CAMBODIA

Hanoi
Vientiane
LAOS
VIETNAM

N. KOREA
Pyongyang
Seoul
S. KOREA

JAPAN
Tokyo

40° N
60° N

9
8

T'aipei
TAIWAN

PHILIPPINES
Manila ■

Kuala Lumpur   MALAYSIA
Putrajaya
SINGAPORE

I N D O N E S I A

Jakarta ■

Tropic of Cancer
20° N

Northern
Mariana Is.
(USA)

MARSHALL
ISLANDS

PALAU

FED. STATES OF
MICRONESIA

Equator   0

NAURU

PACIFIC

OCEAN

7
6

KIRIBATI

TUVALU

PAPUA
NEW
GUINEA
Port
Moresby

SOLOMON
ISLANDS

VANUATU

FIJI
Suva

New
Caledonia
(Fr)
Nouméa

5

20° S

Dili
EAST
TIMOR

INDIAN
OCEAN

COMOROS

Antananarivo ■

MADAGASCAR   MAURITIUS

Mogadishu ■

Íles Kerguelen
(Fr)

AUSTRALIA

Tropic of Capricorn

4

Canberra ■

**NEW
ZEALAND**
Wellington ■

40° S

3

SOUTHERN   OCEAN

60° S

Antarctic Circle

A N T A R C T I C A   H   I   J   80° S

40° E   80° E   120° E   160° E

2

London
12.00 (noon)

The clocks show the time
in a selection of major
world capital cities when
it is noon (Greenwich
Mean Time) in London.

Tokyo
9.00pm

Riyadh
3.00pm

Jakarta
7.00pm

Cape Town
2.00pm

Canberra
10.00pm

Number of countries

200
180   2008
160
140
120
100
80   1950
60
40
20
0

Number of countries in the world

Total world population
6671 million

Largest country
Russian Federation 17 million sq km

Country with most people
China 1 328 million

World's newest countries
Montenegro, Serbia (2006)

Land area
Ten largest countries

18
16
14
12
10
8
6
4
2
0

Million square kilometres

Russian Federation
Canada
U.S.A.
China
Brazil
Australia
India
Argentina
Kazakhstan
Sudan

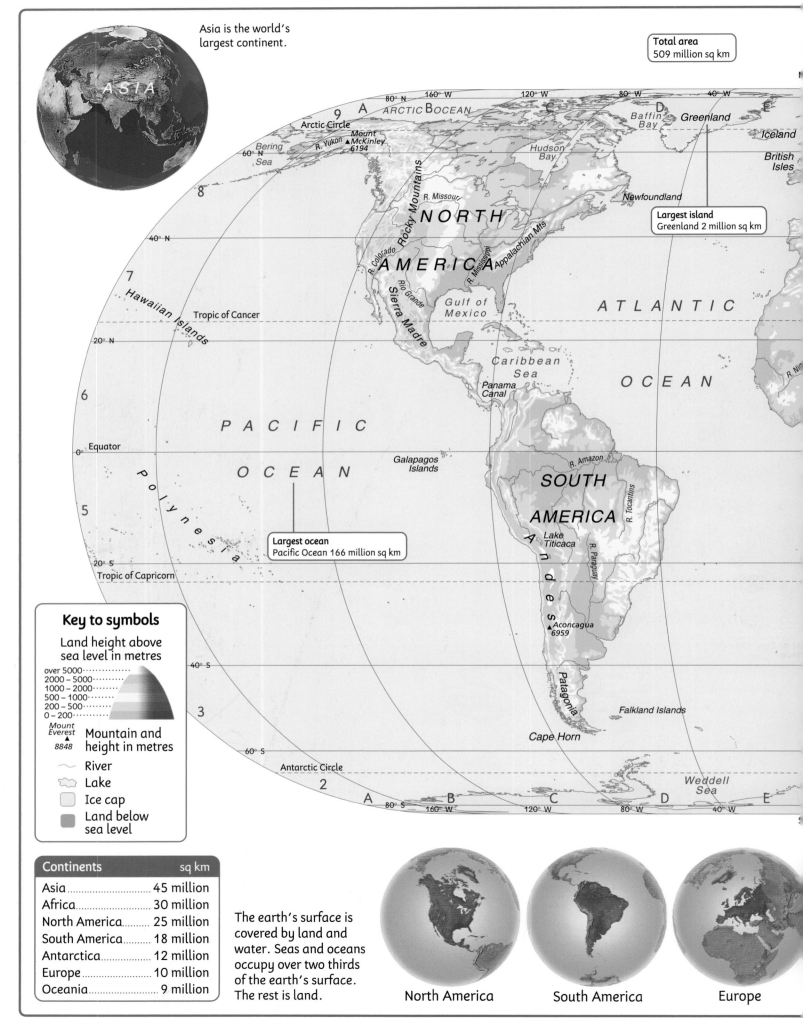

Asia is the world's largest continent.

Total area
509 million sq km

Largest island
Greenland 2 million sq km

Largest ocean
Pacific Ocean 166 million sq km

Key to symbols

Land height above sea level in metres

over 5000
2000 – 5000
1000 – 2000
500 – 1000
200 – 500
0 – 200

Mount Everest ▲
8848
Mountain and height in metres

～ River

Lake

Ice cap

Land below sea level

Continents	sq km
Asia	45 million
Africa	30 million
North America	25 million
South America	18 million
Antarctica	12 million
Europe	10 million
Oceania	9 million

The earth's surface is covered by land and water. Seas and oceans occupy over two thirds of the earth's surface. The rest is land.

North America   South America   Europe

0   850   1700   2550   3400 km

Scale : One centimetre on this map is the same as 850 kilometres on the ground.

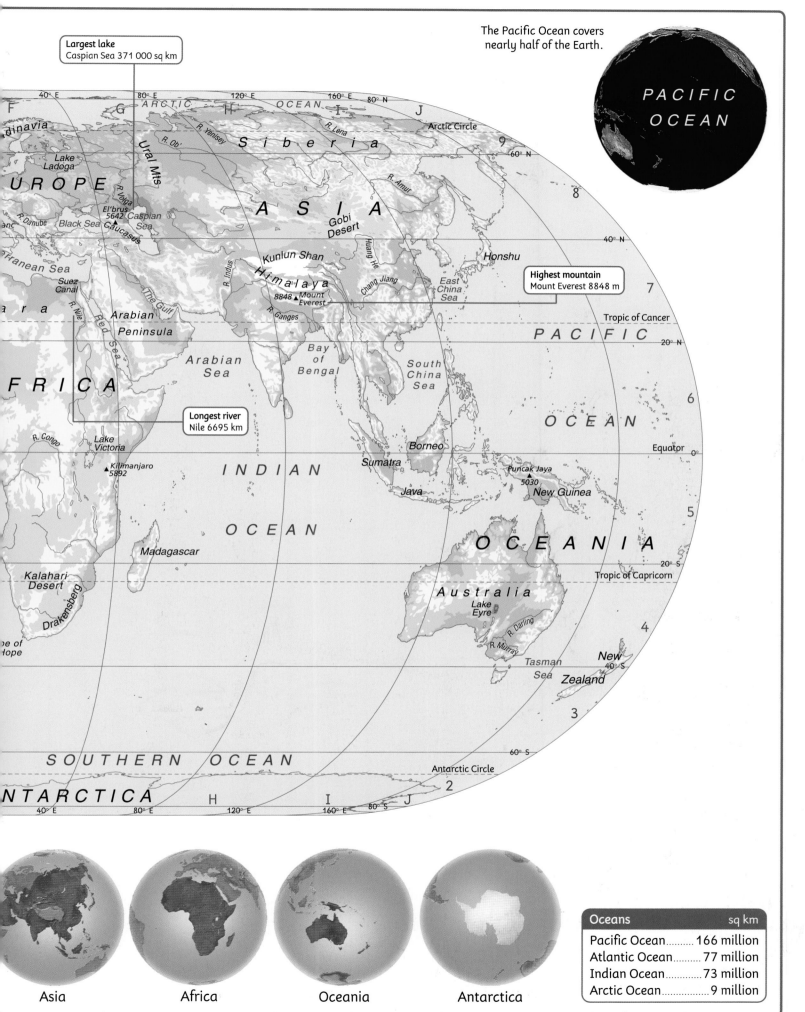

Largest lake
Caspian Sea 371 000 sq km

The Pacific Ocean covers
nearly half of the Earth.

PACIFIC
OCEAN

F
G
ARCTIC
OCEAN
H
I
J
80° N
Arctic Circle
9
60° N
8
40° E
80° E
120° E
160° E

dinavia
Siberia
ASIA
R. Ob
R. Yenisey
R. Lena
R. Amur

Lake
Ladoga
Ural Mts
EUROPE
R. Volga
El'brus
5642
Caspian
Sea
Black Sea
Caucasus
Gobi
Desert
Honshu
40° N

R. Danube
c
Kunlun Shan
Huang He
East
China
Sea
Highest mountain
Mount Everest 8848 m
7

Iranean Sea
Suez
Canal
The Gulf
R. Indus
Himalaya
Chang Jiang
Tropic of Cancer

ra
R. Nile
Arabian
8848
Mount
Everest
20° N

AFRICA
Red Sea
Arabian
Peninsula
Arabian
Sea
R. Ganges
Bay
of
Bengal
South
China
Sea
PACIFIC

OCEAN
6

R. Congo
Lake
Victoria
Longest river
Nile 6695 km
Borneo
Equator
0°

Kilimanjaro
5892
INDIAN
Sumatra
Java
Puncak Jaya
5030
New Guinea
Equator

OCEAN
Madagascar
OCEANIA
5

Kalahari
Desert
Drakensberg
Australia
Lake
Eyre
R. Darling
Tropic of Capricorn
20° S

pe of
Hope
R. Murray
Tasman
Sea
New
Zealand
40° S
4

3
SOUTHERN
OCEAN
60° S
Antarctic Circle
2

ANTARCTICA
H
I
J
80° S
40° E
80° E
120° E
160° E

Asia

Africa

Oceania

Antarctica

Oceans	sq km
Pacific Ocean	166 million
Atlantic Ocean	77 million
Indian Ocean	73 million
Arctic Ocean	9 million

Climate graphs

The red line shows average temperature.
The blue bars show average monthly rainfall.

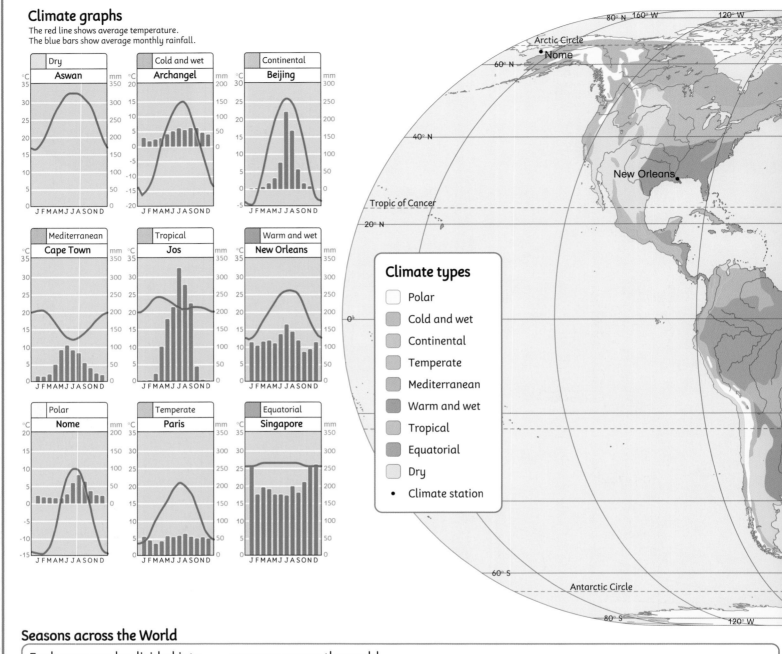

Climate types
- Polar
- Cold and wet
- Continental
- Temperate
- Mediterranean
- Warm and wet
- Tropical
- Equatorial
- Dry
- • Climate station

Seasons across the World

Each year can be divided into seasons. The dials below show how the length of each season can vary across the world depending on the distance from the equator.

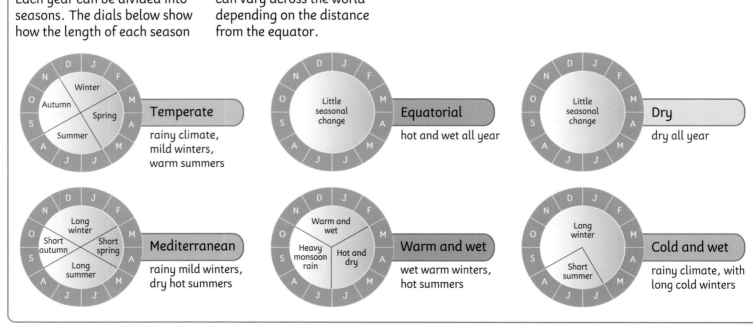

Temperate
rainy climate, mild winters, warm summers

Equatorial
hot and wet all year

Dry
dry all year

Mediterranean
rainy mild winters, dry hot summers

Warm and wet
wet warm winters, hot summers

Cold and wet
rainy climate, with long cold winters

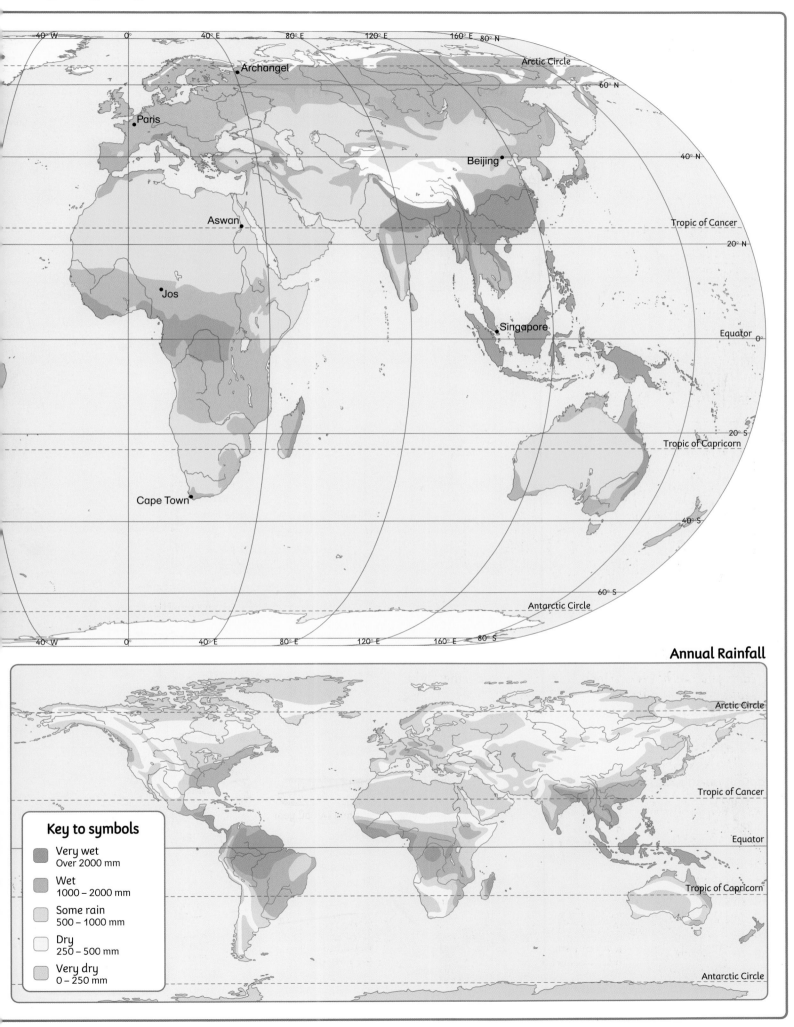

Annual Rainfall

Key to symbols

- **Very wet**
  Over 2000 mm
- **Wet**
  1000 – 2000 mm
- **Some rain**
  500 – 1000 mm
- **Dry**
  250 – 500 mm
- **Very dry**
  0 – 250 mm

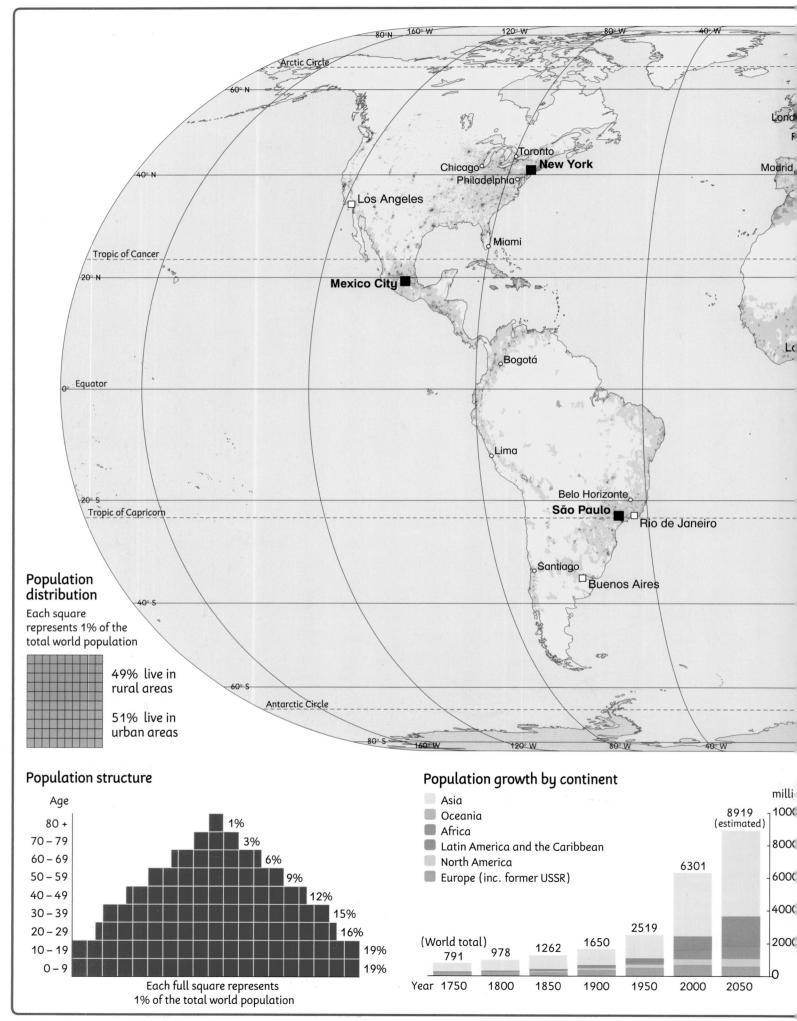

Population distribution

Each square represents 1% of the total world population

49% live in rural areas

51% live in urban areas

Cities (map labels):
Toronto, Chicago, **New York**, Philadelphia, Los Angeles, Miami, **Mexico City**, Bogotá, Lima, Belo Horizonte, **São Paulo**, Rio de Janeiro, Santiago, Buenos Aires, Lond..., Madrid, Lo...

Latitude/longitude labels:
Arctic Circle, 60° N, 40° N, Tropic of Cancer, 20° N, Equator, 20° S, Tropic of Capricorn, 40° S, 60° S, Antarctic Circle, 80° N, 160° W, 120° W, 80° W, 40° W

Population structure

Age

80 +	1%
70 – 79	3%
60 – 69	6%
50 – 59	9%
40 – 49	12%
30 – 39	15%
20 – 29	16%
10 – 19	19%
0 – 9	19%

Each full square represents 1% of the total world population

Population growth by continent

milli...

Asia
Oceania
Africa
Latin America and the Caribbean
North America
Europe (inc. former USSR)

(World total)

Year	1750	1800	1850	1900	1950	2000	2050
	791	978	1262	1650	2519	6301	8919 (estimated)

1000
8000
6000
4000
2000
0

0 1000 2000 3000 4000 km

Scale : One centimetre on this map is the same as 850 kilometres on the ground.

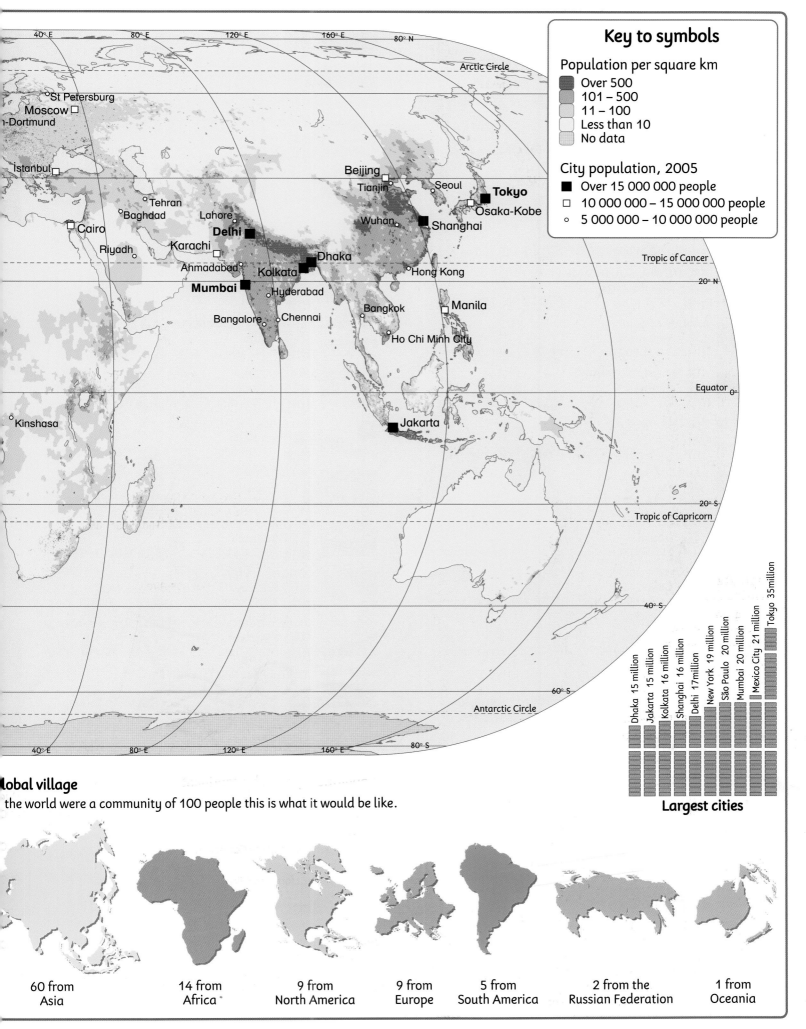

Key to symbols

Population per square km

- Over 500
- 101 – 500
- 11 – 100
- Less than 10
- No data

City population, 2005

- ■ Over 15 000 000 people
- □ 10 000 000 – 15 000 000 people
- ○ 5 000 000 – 10 000 000 people

Arctic Circle

St Petersburg
Moscow
-Dortmund
İstanbul
Tehran
Baghdad
Cairo
Riyadh
Lahore
Karachi
Delhi
Ahmadabad
Mumbai
Kolkata
Hyderabad
Bangalore
Chennai
Dhaka
Beijing
Tianjin
Seoul
Tokyo
Osaka-Kobe
Wuhan
Shanghai
Hong Kong
Bangkok
Manila
Ho Chi Minh City
Jakarta
Kinshasa

Tropic of Cancer
20° N
Equator 0°
Tropic of Capricorn
20° S
40° S
60° S
Antarctic Circle
80° S

Largest cities

- Dhaka 15 million
- Jakarta 15 million
- Kolkata 16 million
- Shanghai 16 million
- Delhi 17 million
- New York 19 million
- São Paulo 20 million
- Mumbai 20 million
- Mexico City 21 million
- Tokyo 35 million

Global village

If the world were a community of 100 people this is what it would be like.

| 60 from Asia | 14 from Africa | 9 from North America | 9 from Europe | 5 from South America | 2 from the Russian Federation | 1 from Oceania |

Flag	COUNTRY, CONTINENT 🏛 Capital City 👥 Population	Area square kilometres

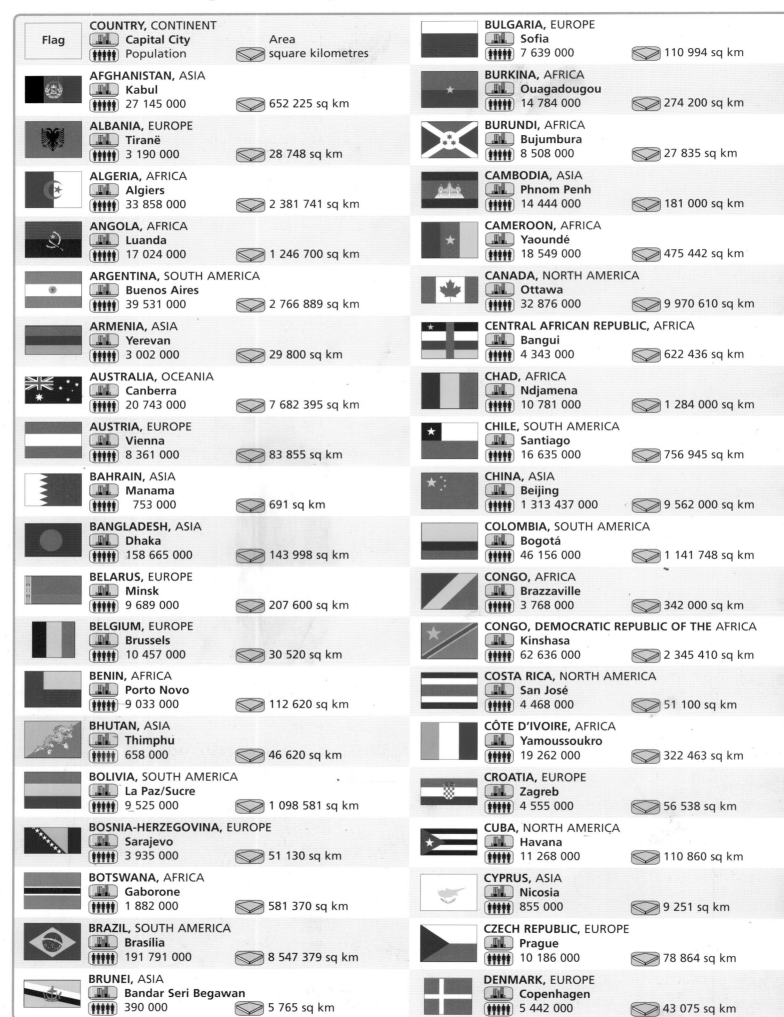

AFGHANISTAN, ASIA
🏛 Kabul
👥 27 145 000 — 652 225 sq km

ALBANIA, EUROPE
🏛 Tiranë
👥 3 190 000 — 28 748 sq km

ALGERIA, AFRICA
🏛 Algiers
👥 33 858 000 — 2 381 741 sq km

ANGOLA, AFRICA
🏛 Luanda
👥 17 024 000 — 1 246 700 sq km

ARGENTINA, SOUTH AMERICA
🏛 Buenos Aires
👥 39 531 000 — 2 766 889 sq km

ARMENIA, ASIA
🏛 Yerevan
👥 3 002 000 — 29 800 sq km

AUSTRALIA, OCEANIA
🏛 Canberra
👥 20 743 000 — 7 682 395 sq km

AUSTRIA, EUROPE
🏛 Vienna
👥 8 361 000 — 83 855 sq km

BAHRAIN, ASIA
🏛 Manama
👥 753 000 — 691 sq km

BANGLADESH, ASIA
🏛 Dhaka
👥 158 665 000 — 143 998 sq km

BELARUS, EUROPE
🏛 Minsk
👥 9 689 000 — 207 600 sq km

BELGIUM, EUROPE
🏛 Brussels
👥 10 457 000 — 30 520 sq km

BENIN, AFRICA
🏛 Porto Novo
👥 9 033 000 — 112 620 sq km

BHUTAN, ASIA
🏛 Thimphu
👥 658 000 — 46 620 sq km

BOLIVIA, SOUTH AMERICA
🏛 La Paz/Sucre
👥 9 525 000 — 1 098 581 sq km

BOSNIA-HERZEGOVINA, EUROPE
🏛 Sarajevo
👥 3 935 000 — 51 130 sq km

BOTSWANA, AFRICA
🏛 Gaborone
👥 1 882 000 — 581 370 sq km

BRAZIL, SOUTH AMERICA
🏛 Brasília
👥 191 791 000 — 8 547 379 sq km

BRUNEI, ASIA
🏛 Bandar Seri Begawan
👥 390 000 — 5 765 sq km

BULGARIA, EUROPE
🏛 Sofia
👥 7 639 000 — 110 994 sq km

BURKINA, AFRICA
🏛 Ouagadougou
👥 14 784 000 — 274 200 sq km

BURUNDI, AFRICA
🏛 Bujumbura
👥 8 508 000 — 27 835 sq km

CAMBODIA, ASIA
🏛 Phnom Penh
👥 14 444 000 — 181 000 sq km

CAMEROON, AFRICA
🏛 Yaoundé
👥 18 549 000 — 475 442 sq km

CANADA, NORTH AMERICA
🏛 Ottawa
👥 32 876 000 — 9 970 610 sq km

CENTRAL AFRICAN REPUBLIC, AFRICA
🏛 Bangui
👥 4 343 000 — 622 436 sq km

CHAD, AFRICA
🏛 Ndjamena
👥 10 781 000 — 1 284 000 sq km

CHILE, SOUTH AMERICA
🏛 Santiago
👥 16 635 000 — 756 945 sq km

CHINA, ASIA
🏛 Beijing
👥 1 313 437 000 — 9 562 000 sq km

COLOMBIA, SOUTH AMERICA
🏛 Bogotá
👥 46 156 000 — 1 141 748 sq km

CONGO, AFRICA
🏛 Brazzaville
👥 3 768 000 — 342 000 sq km

CONGO, DEMOCRATIC REPUBLIC OF THE AFRICA
🏛 Kinshasa
👥 62 636 000 — 2 345 410 sq km

COSTA RICA, NORTH AMERICA
🏛 San José
👥 4 468 000 — 51 100 sq km

CÔTE D'IVOIRE, AFRICA
🏛 Yamoussoukro
👥 19 262 000 — 322 463 sq km

CROATIA, EUROPE
🏛 Zagreb
👥 4 555 000 — 56 538 sq km

CUBA, NORTH AMERICA
🏛 Havana
👥 11 268 000 — 110 860 sq km

CYPRUS, ASIA
🏛 Nicosia
👥 855 000 — 9 251 sq km

CZECH REPUBLIC, EUROPE
🏛 Prague
👥 10 186 000 — 78 864 sq km

DENMARK, EUROPE
🏛 Copenhagen
👥 5 442 000 — 43 075 sq km

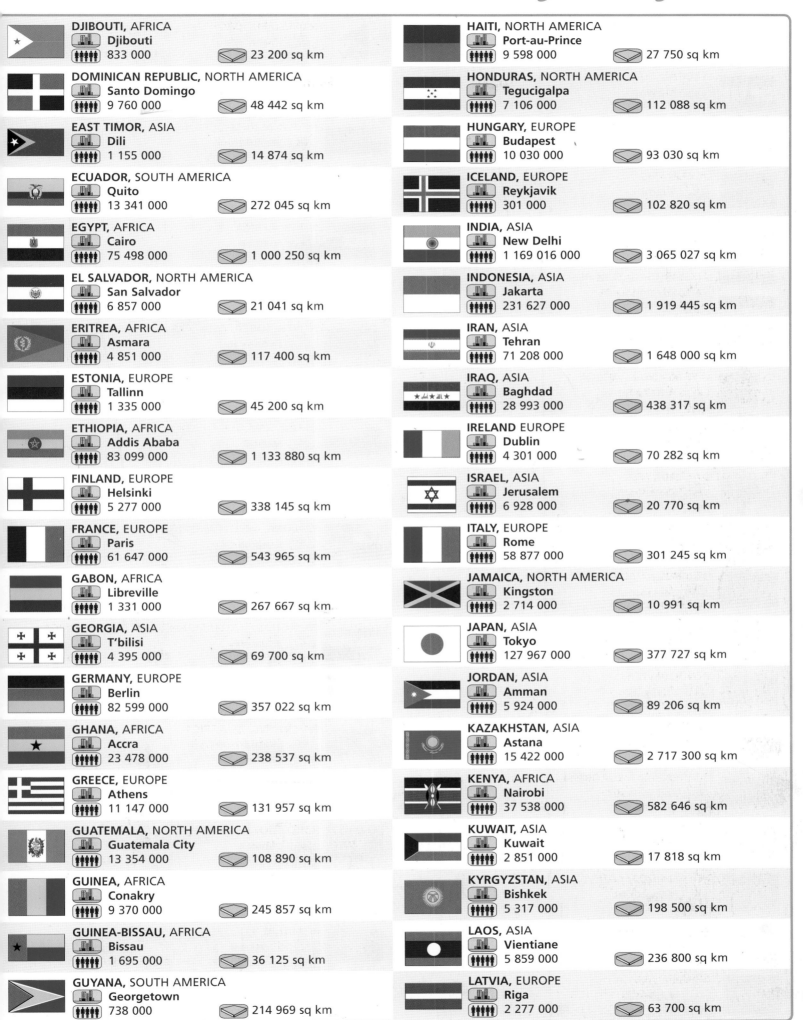

DJIBOUTI, AFRICA
Djibouti
833 000 — 23 200 sq km

DOMINICAN REPUBLIC, NORTH AMERICA
Santo Domingo
9 760 000 — 48 442 sq km

EAST TIMOR, ASIA
Dili
1 155 000 — 14 874 sq km

ECUADOR, SOUTH AMERICA
Quito
13 341 000 — 272 045 sq km

EGYPT, AFRICA
Cairo
75 498 000 — 1 000 250 sq km

EL SALVADOR, NORTH AMERICA
San Salvador
6 857 000 — 21 041 sq km

ERITREA, AFRICA
Asmara
4 851 000 — 117 400 sq km

ESTONIA, EUROPE
Tallinn
1 335 000 — 45 200 sq km

ETHIOPIA, AFRICA
Addis Ababa
83 099 000 — 1 133 880 sq km

FINLAND, EUROPE
Helsinki
5 277 000 — 338 145 sq km

FRANCE, EUROPE
Paris
61 647 000 — 543 965 sq km

GABON, AFRICA
Libreville
1 331 000 — 267 667 sq km

GEORGIA, ASIA
T'bilisi
4 395 000 — 69 700 sq km

GERMANY, EUROPE
Berlin
82 599 000 — 357 022 sq km

GHANA, AFRICA
Accra
23 478 000 — 238 537 sq km

GREECE, EUROPE
Athens
11 147 000 — 131 957 sq km

GUATEMALA, NORTH AMERICA
Guatemala City
13 354 000 — 108 890 sq km

GUINEA, AFRICA
Conakry
9 370 000 — 245 857 sq km

GUINEA-BISSAU, AFRICA
Bissau
1 695 000 — 36 125 sq km

GUYANA, SOUTH AMERICA
Georgetown
738 000 — 214 969 sq km

HAITI, NORTH AMERICA
Port-au-Prince
9 598 000 — 27 750 sq km

HONDURAS, NORTH AMERICA
Tegucigalpa
7 106 000 — 112 088 sq km

HUNGARY, EUROPE
Budapest
10 030 000 — 93 030 sq km

ICELAND, EUROPE
Reykjavik
301 000 — 102 820 sq km

INDIA, ASIA
New Delhi
1 169 016 000 — 3 065 027 sq km

INDONESIA, ASIA
Jakarta
231 627 000 — 1 919 445 sq km

IRAN, ASIA
Tehran
71 208 000 — 1 648 000 sq km

IRAQ, ASIA
Baghdad
28 993 000 — 438 317 sq km

IRELAND EUROPE
Dublin
4 301 000 — 70 282 sq km

ISRAEL, ASIA
Jerusalem
6 928 000 — 20 770 sq km

ITALY, EUROPE
Rome
58 877 000 — 301 245 sq km

JAMAICA, NORTH AMERICA
Kingston
2 714 000 — 10 991 sq km

JAPAN, ASIA
Tokyo
127 967 000 — 377 727 sq km

JORDAN, ASIA
Amman
5 924 000 — 89 206 sq km

KAZAKHSTAN, ASIA
Astana
15 422 000 — 2 717 300 sq km

KENYA, AFRICA
Nairobi
37 538 000 — 582 646 sq km

KUWAIT, ASIA
Kuwait
2 851 000 — 17 818 sq km

KYRGYZSTAN, ASIA
Bishkek
5 317 000 — 198 500 sq km

LAOS, ASIA
Vientiane
5 859 000 — 236 800 sq km

LATVIA, EUROPE
Riga
2 277 000 — 63 700 sq km

LEBANON, ASIA
Beirut
4 099 000
10 452 sq km

LESOTHO, AFRICA
Maseru
2 008 000
30 355 sq km

LIBERIA, AFRICA
Monrovia
3 750 000
111 369 sq km

LIBYA, AFRICA
Tripoli
6 160 000
1 759 540 sq km

LITHUANIA, EUROPE
Vilnius
3 390 000
65 200 sq km

LUXEMBOURG, EUROPE
Luxembourg
467 000
2 586 sq km

MACEDONIA (F.Y.R.O.M.), EUROPE
Skopje
2 038 000
25 713 sq km

MADAGASCAR, AFRICA
Antananarivo
19 683 000
587 041 sq km

MALAWI, AFRICA
Lilongwe
13 925 000
118 484 sq km

MALAYSIA, ASIA
Kuala Lumpur/Putrajaya
26 572 000
332 965 sq km

MALI, AFRICA
Bamako
12 337 000
1 240 140 sq km

MAURITANIA, AFRICA
Nouakchott
3 124 000
1 030 700 sq km

MEXICO, NORTH AMERICA
Mexico City
106 535 000
1 972 545 sq km

MOLDOVA, EUROPE
Chişinău
3 794 000
33 700 sq km

MONGOLIA, ASIA
Ulan Bator
2 629 000
1 565 000 sq km

MONTENEGRO, EUROPE
Podgorica
598 000
13 812 sq km

MOROCCO, AFRICA
Rabat
31 224 000
446 550 sq km

MOZAMBIQUE, AFRICA
Maputo
21 397 000
799 380 sq km

MYANMAR (BURMA), ASIA
Nay Pyi Taw/Yangon
48 798 000
676 577 sq km

NAMIBIA, AFRICA
Windhoek
2 074 000
824 292 sq km

NEPAL, ASIA
Kathmandu
28 196 000
147 181 sq km

NETHERLANDS, EUROPE
Amsterdam/The Hague
16 419 000
41 526 sq km

NEW ZEALAND, OCEANIA
Wellington
4 179 000
270 534 sq km

NICARAGUA, NORTH AMERICA
Managua
5 603 000
130 000 sq km

NIGER, AFRICA
Niamey
14 226 000
1 267 000 sq km

NIGERIA, AFRICA
Abuja
148 093 000
923 768 sq km

NORTH KOREA, ASIA
Pyongyang
23 790 000
120 538 sq km

NORWAY, EUROPE
Oslo
4 698 000
323 878 sq km

OMAN, ASIA
Muscat
2 595 000
309 500 sq km

PAKISTAN, ASIA
Islamabad
163 902 000
803 940 sq km

PANAMA, NORTH AMERICA
Panama City
3 343 000
77 082 sq km

PAPUA NEW GUINEA, OCEANIA
Port Moresby
6 331 000
462 840 sq km

PARAGUAY, SOUTH AMERICA
Asunción
6 127 000
406 752 sq km

PERU, SOUTH AMERICA
Lima
27 903 000
1 285 216 sq km

PHILIPPINES, ASIA
Manila
87 960 000
300 000 sq km

POLAND, EUROPE
Warsaw
38 082 000
312 683 sq km

PORTUGAL, EUROPE
Lisbon
10 623 000
88 940 sq km

QATAR, ASIA
Doha
841 000
11 437 sq km

ROMANIA, EUROPE
Bucharest
21 438 000
237 500 sq km

RUSSIAN FEDERATION, EUROPE/ASIA
Moscow
142 499 000
17 075 400 sq km

SAUDI ARABIA, ASIA
Riyadh
24 735 000
2 200 000 sq km

SENEGAL, AFRICA
Dakar
12 379 000
196 720 sq km

SERBIA, EUROPE
Belgrade
9 858 000
88 361 sq km

SIERRA LEONE, AFRICA
Freetown
5 866 000
71 740 sq km

SINGAPORE, ASIA
Singapore
4 436 000
639 sq km

SLOVAKIA, EUROPE
Bratislava
5 390 000
49 035 sq km

SLOVENIA, EUROPE
Ljubljana
2 002 000
20 251 sq km

SOMALIA, AFRICA
Mogadishu
8 699 000
637 657 sq km

SOUTH AFRICA, REPUBLIC OF, AFRICA
Pretoria/Cape Town
48 577 000
1 219 080 sq km

SOUTH KOREA, ASIA
Seoul
48 224 000
99 274 sq km

SPAIN, EUROPE
Madrid
44 279 000
504 782 sq km

SRI LANKA, ASIA
Sri Jayewardenepura Kotte
19 299 000
65 610 sq km

SUDAN, AFRICA
Khartoum
38 560 000
2 505 813 sq km

SURINAME, SOUTH AMERICA
Paramaribo
458 000
163 820 sq km

SWAZILAND, AFRICA
Mbabane
1 141 000
17 364 sq km

SWEDEN, EUROPE
Stockholm
9 119 000
449 964 sq km

SWITZERLAND, EUROPE
Bern
7 484 000
41 293 sq km

SYRIA, ASIA
Damascus
19 929 000
185 180 sq km

TAIWAN, ASIA
T'aipei
22 880 000
36 179 sq km

TAJIKISTAN, ASIA
Dushanbe
6 736 000
143 100 sq km

TANZANIA, AFRICA
Dodoma
40 454 000
945 087 sq km

THAILAND, ASIA
Bangkok
63 884 000
513 115 sq km

THE GAMBIA, AFRICA
Banjul
1 709 000
11 295 sq km

TOGO, AFRICA
Lomé
6 585 000
56 785 sq km

TRINIDAD AND TOBAGO, SOUTH AMERICA
Port of Spain
1 333 000
5 130 sq km

TUNISIA, AFRICA
Tunis
10 327 000
164 150 sq km

TURKEY, ASIA/EUROPE
Ankara
74 877 000
779 452 sq km

TURKMENISTAN, ASIA
Ashgabat
4 965 000
488 100 sq km

UGANDA, AFRICA
Kampala
30 884 000
241 038 sq km

UKRAINE, EUROPE
Kiev
46 205 000
603 700 sq km

UNITED ARAB EMIRATES, ASIA
Abu Dhabi
4 380 000
77 700 sq km

UNITED KINGDOM, EUROPE
London
60 769 000
243 609 sq km

UNITED STATES OF AMERICA, NORTH AMERICA
Washington
305 826 000
9 809 378 sq km

URUGUAY, SOUTH AMERICA
Montevideo
3 340 000
176 215 sq km

UZBEKISTAN, ASIA
Tashkent
27 372 000
447 400 sq km

VENEZUELA, SOUTH AMERICA
Caracas
27 657 000
912 050 sq km

VIETNAM, ASIA
Hanoi
87 375 000
329 565 sq km

YEMEN, ASIA
San'a
22 389 000
527 968 sq km

ZAMBIA, AFRICA
Lusaka
11 922 000
752 614 sq km

ZIMBABWE, AFRICA
Harare
13 349 000
390 759 sq km

68 Index